Tarot in the Land of Mystereum

An Imagination Primer
Jordan Hoggard

4880 Lower Valley Road · Atglen, Pennsylvania 19310

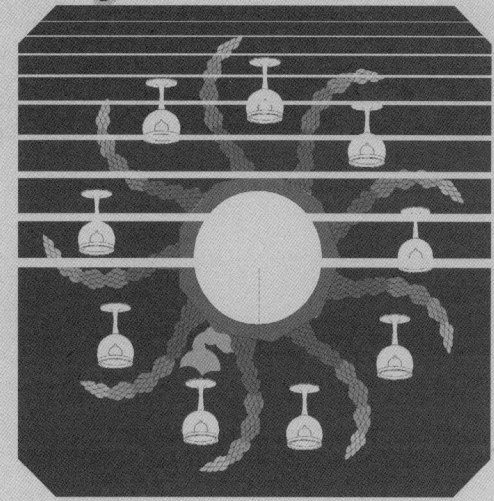

Schiffer Books are available at special discounts for bulk purchases for sales promotions or premiums. Special editions, including personalized covers, corporate imprints, and excerpts can be created in large quantities for special needs. For more information contact the publisher:

Published by Schiffer Publishing Ltd.
4880 Lower Valley Road
Atglen, PA 19310
Phone: (610) 593-1777; Fax: (610) 593-2002
E-mail: Info@schifferbooks.com

For the largest selection of fine reference books on this and related subjects, please visit our web site at
www.schifferbooks.com

We are always looking for people to write books on new and related subjects. If you have an idea for a book please contact us at the above address.

This book may be purchased from the publisher.
Include $5.00 for shipping.
Please try your bookstore first.
You may write for a free catalog.

In Europe, Schiffer books are distributed by
Bushwood Books
6 Marksbury Ave.
Kew Gardens
Surrey TW9 4JF England
Phone: 44 (0) 20 8392-8585; Fax: 44 (0) 20 8392-9876
E-mail: info@bushwoodbooks.co.uk
Website: www.bushwoodbooks.co.uk

All Text and artwork by Jordan Hoggard

Copyright © 2010 Jordan Hoggard
Library of Congress Control Number: 2010935181

All rights reserved. No part of this work may be reproduced or used in any form or by any means—graphic, electronic, or mechanical, including photocopying or information storage and retrieval systems—without written permission from the publisher.
The scanning, uploading and distribution of this book or any part thereof via the Internet or via any other means without the permission of the publisher is illegal and punishable by law. Please purchase only authorized editions and do not participate in or encourage the electronic piracy of copyrighted materials.
"Schiffer," "Schiffer Publishing Ltd. & Design," and the "Design of pen and ink well" are registered trademarks of Schiffer Publishing Ltd.

Designed by RoS
Type set in Americana BT/Souvenir Lt BT

ISBN: 978-0-7643-3601-0

Printed in China

Dedication

For your imagination to soar and root. A portrait of yesterday, for those who are not tomorrow... To your inner inheritances and imagination, inner treasures present when you were born.

May you remember, may you dream. Each birth brilliant in its age, may you discover all your life.

Acknowledgments

Susan B. Hale. You gave me two lithographs when I was three months old. I cherish them. They have lived with me since.

Contents

Welcome 6
Some Basic Ideas to Begin With .. 12

Part One
Archetypal Imagination
THE FOOL'S JOURNEY THROUGH THE MAJOR ARCANA

    Ø THE FOOL ∞ 15
    I THE MAGICIAN 18
    II THE HIGH PRIESTESS 20
    III THE EMPRESS 23
    IV THE EMPEROR 25
    V THE HIEROPHANT 27
    VI THE LOVERS 29
    VII THE CHARIOT 32
    VIII JUSTICE 34
    IX THE HERMIT 37
    X THE WHEEL 40
    XI STRENGTH 42
    XII THE HANGED MAN 45
    XIII DEATH 48
    XIV TEMPERANCE 50
    XV THE DEVIL 53
    XVI THE TOWER 56
    XVII THE STAR 59
    XVIII THE MOON 62
    XIX THE SUN 64
    XX JUDGMENT 66
    XXI THE WORLD 69

Part Two
Grounding Imagination
THE FOOL'S JOURNEY THROUGH PENTACLES

    THE ACE OF PENTACLES 73
    THE 2 OF PENTACLES 75
    THE 3 OF PENTACLES 77
    THE 4 OF PENTACLES 79
    THE 5 OF PENTACLES 80
    THE 6 OF PENTACLES 83
    THE 7 OF PENTACLES 85
    THE 8 OF PENTACLES 87
    THE 9 OF PENTACLES 89
    THE 10 OF PENTACLES 91
    THE PAGE OF PENTACLES 93
    THE KNIGHT OF PENTACLES 95
    THE QUEEN OF PENTACLES 97
    THE KING OF PENTACLES 99

Part Three
Fulfilling Imagination
THE FOOL'S JOURNEY THROUGH CUPS

    THE ACE OF CUPS 102
    THE 2 OF CUPS 103

THE 3 OF CUPS 105
THE 4 OF CUPS 107
THE 5 OF CUPS 109
THE 6 OF CUPS 111
THE 7 OF CUPS 112
THE 8 OF CUPS 114
THE 9 OF CUPS 116
THE 10 OF CUPS 117
THE PAGE OF CUPS 119
THE KNIGHT OF CUPS 120
THE QUEEN OF CUPS 122
THE KING OF CUPS 123

Part Four
Energizing Imagination
THE FOOL'S JOURNEY THROUGH WANDS

THE ACE OF WANDS 127
THE 2 OF WANDS 129
THE 3 OF WANDS 131
THE 4 OF WANDS 132
THE 5 OF WANDS 134
THE 6 OF WANDS 136
THE 7 OF WANDS 137
THE 8 OF WANDS 139
THE 9 OF WANDS 140
THE 10 OF WANDS 142
THE PAGE OF WANDS 143
THE KNIGHT OF WANDS 145
THE QUEEN OF WANDS 146
THE KING OF WANDS 148

Part Five
Communicative Imagination
THE FOOL'S JOURNEY THROUGH SWORDS

THE ACE OF SWORDS 151
THE 2 OF SWORDS 154
THE 3 OF SWORDS 156
THE 4 OF SWORDS 158
THE 5 OF SWORDS 159
THE 6 OF SWORDS 161
THE 7 OF SWORDS 163
THE 8 OF SWORDS 165
THE 9 OF SWORDS 167
THE 10 OF SWORDS 169
THE PAGE OF SWORDS 170
THE KNIGHT OF SWORDS 172
THE QUEEN OF SWORDS 173
THE KING OF SWORDS 175

Appendix
Imagination Tool Cheat Sheet 178

About the Author 192

Welcome

Meditate Your Contemplation
Contemplate Your Meditation

Card Back
Meditation, contemplation, centering

Welcome to The Land of Mystereum! Welcome to a journey of creativity and imagination where you are the guide. Just imagine it, and it will be so! In the Land of Mystereum we will help you establish harmonious relationships with your ideas and feelings. We will explore identity and personality with ideas. There are things present here that will help you guide your intuition and imagination. Your intuition and imagination are the voice and place of your inner essence and your gut instincts. Intuition and imagination can help you work with your memories and ideas and dreams. You and your intuition will be the ultimate guide here as you explore. Your past, your ideas, and the dreams for your future can come together here in The Land of Mystereum. We are all similar. We are also each very unique! We celebrate our differences. "All similar, each unique," is our motto. It keeps our lives lively!

We would all like to encourage you to think of a mermaid or merman as your intuition's companion or muse. Or, make up your own Mystereum companion. We feel that this will help you to sense and focus on the personality of your thoughts and ideas. Your bright light shines from your identity through your personality. We invite you to imagine that your ideas are as bright as stars and sunlight!

Big places and small places and all places and scales in between are here in the Land of Mystereum. We like to help you help yourself keep your intuition and imagination fresh and active in everything you do. Use your imagination here to open new pathways of creativity. They can lead you to make enthusiastic new places along the way! All the while we like to celebrate qualities that you already have. Use the qualities of your imagination all along the way to complete your tasks while you play.

Here in The Land of Mystereum each of us will gift you something we call *Imagination Tools*. Mystereum is here to gift you a place to practice with your intuition and imagination to strengthen all of your senses. The big gift here is to help you develop a powerful and aware witness as part of your journey as you see, sense, feel, and do things that are important to you. You can also use this powerful witness as a helper to prime and develop your imagination. The Land of Mystereum was created as an Imagination Primer.

In Mystereum you can unfold and inform your journey as often and in as many ways as you please. We recommend to practice with your imagination often. Regular use, or ritual use, of your intuition and imagination can strengthen the discipline and strength of your creative abilities. We find that the discipline of the ritual makes even the most complex ideas very manageable over time. Sometimes you even comprehend complex things right off the bat!

THE FOOL will lead you into the Land of Mystereum. Each of us is represented by THE FOOL where we narrate and live our lives. You can also BE THE FOOL as you lead your own way! Read THE FOOL's story out loud in your own voice. Then, POOF, it is yours to use and direct your journey on each path you choose!

THE FOOL first started on a journey in Mystereum before there was a map. To keep the journey fresh, THE FOOL became comfortable with the unknown. In Mystereum, we like to say that THE FOOL became comfortable with the *not-knowing*. The *not-knowing* means that the meanings and reasons along the way occur in your actions rather than in explanation. This idea of *not-knowing* is based on your experience. Think of the *not-knowing* as your own personal ability to be pleasantly surprised as you have original thoughts. So think of the *not-knowing* as your own personal ability to be pleasantly surprised as your ideas add their own qualities to the mix of your imagination. Think of the *not-knowing* as a way to open doors to discovery. We like to think about your imagination as a place of constant discovery!

We have made every effort to make *Tarot in the Land of Mystereum* simple and easy to use. Mystereum has 79 unique places. There are 78 cards plus a card back. Each card is the home of a Mystereum Tarot character and has two chapters here. In the first chapter of each card there is a picture of the Mystereum Tarot character that you can use as a visual guide. We recommend that you focus on each image, breathe, and see what you see, sense what you feel. The picture page also has a description of some of what the card indicates. You can use this to learn more about each card's character and place. You will also find other great meanings in places outside of Mystereum. You are encouraged to explore and tailor and modify anything you please as you go along. Tune and tailor your perspective when you feel you would like to do so!

The second chapter for each card gets fun! Each Mystereum Tarot character speaks to you in their own voice. We suggest that you read these out loud. Each card also has something for you. Some have single gifts. Some have packages. We call these gifts Imagination Tools.

We only ask two things of you in Mystereum. First, look into each card's picture and sense what comes to mind before you read. Spend a little time and simply breathe with the image as you let your eyes take a visual field trip around the card's portrait. Then, when you feel ready to do so, say what you are feeling out loud to yourself. We do this when we see and feel things. It is how we practice to get ready to express things clearly. Some feelings settle into our actions and become natural in the things we do. Sometimes feelings are so clear that we express things right off the bat! Sometimes we think and sense a great deal with them first.

The second thing we ask of you? We ask you to practice and think about, sense, and develop your ideas with the Imagination Tools each card gifts you. Over time we feel that the Imagination Tools you receive for your intuition and imagination will help you help yourself to become a further whiz with your ideas! We like things to strengthen both work and play, both mind and body. We make discoveries at both work and in play. To us, imagination is for everything.

Enjoy The Land of Mystereum! All of the characters take it from here. You see, I am the book cover and binding to you. I like to be alive, too. Pardon taking so long to tell you who I was. All of the other Mystereum characters have been inside getting ready for you! Their warm-up and practice is important to make sure everything is ready.

I am the book cover and the binding. You can also call me a vessel. I am a container. I hold and unfold the story as you turn the pages. The Mystereum characters are the contained. They are the content. Each character has their own story to tell, their own unique way to welcome you here. Soon enough you may find that we are each also both container and contained in experience on our journey! We are like alchemy! We are container and contained at one and the same time. Like YOU! We feel that you might just tell us these things in a different way soon after you take a field trip to discover what alchemy is! You might just find some here in The Land of Mystereum, too. Cool thing is, you might be really good at alchemy already.

So, on to the fun! All the Mystereum characters wrote you a note!

Hi There! Glad you are here! Welcome to the Land of Mystereum where imagination expands with vibrant love and wonderful laughter. Friendships are celebrated! There is a ton of great stuff that we have made for you! You will see all of this as you go along. You may even see and make more than we've made. Whatcha say, on to the fun?!

First we will show you *Archetypal Imagination* with a group called the MAJOR ARCANA. That is where big ideas that inspire live. Next, we will move to *Grounding Imagination*. The PENTACLES will speak to you there. They were created last, but afterwards we felt to place them first. We wanted to start with the idea of a ground and a foundation to provide a place for the first steps of your journey here. Grounds and foundations and places are important! And, Oh MY, there are so many types of them! In fact each of us has our own special kind of each. You will see.

With PENTACLES we will help you with idea placement. For now, simply remember that PENTACLES represent the earth and solid things.

Then, we journey to *Fulfilling Imagination* with CUPS and water and flow. With CUPS, we will show how ideas nourish you and your imagination. That is pretty cool to us! For, now simply remember that CUPS represent water and flow.

Energizing Imagination is next! We will use WANDS and fire and energy that activate and invigorate ideas. For now, simply remember that WANDS represent fire and energy.

And then, we will put them all together and journey to *Communicative Imagination* with SWORDS and air. We will work with ideas that come together to be aired and communicated. For now, simply remember that SWORDS represent air and communication.

To keep it simple while mixing in a little more of the good stuff, simply remember:

- *Archetypal Imagination* is about THE MAJOR ARCANA with big ideas.
- *Grounding Imagination* is about PENTACLES with solid things that you can touch.
- *Fulfilling Imagination* is about CUPS with flow and how you feel.

- *Energizing Imagination* is about Wands with energy that invigorates you.
- *Communicative Imagination* is about SWORDS with communication and how you interact.

Here we go! We like to start with a fun exercise. If you have more people, then any flexible circle will work. After this, your homework will be simple. Simply remember to practice regularly and bring your imagination and curiosity and questions with you each time. OHHH, we LOVE questions! We feel there is a creative place in really great questions where things grow well and unfold discoveries!

So, got your imagination and curiosity and a rubber band? Ready for a fun exercise?! Cool Kewel!

Pick up the rubber band and hold it with both hands so it is shaped in a circle.

Slowly, very slowly, twist the circle by rotating your hands opposite directions.

As your circle folds over itself you have made your circle into your own infinity symbol! ∞ How COOL is THAT?!! It is like an 8 on its side. We like it when you smile and laugh and clearly see things as they are as they change and evolve and return.

Slowly turn your infinity back into a circle again, and without stopping. . .very slowly make a circle into infinity and back and forth until you smile and are ready to explore the Land of Mystereum. This idea of the heartbeat of a circle to infinity is your key.

A circle, already with no beginning or end, becomes infinite each time as you transform it at the tips of your fingers with a simple rubber band.

The center is not necessarily in the middle. The center is where you are on your journey. The center where you are is vibrant and alive like when you make a circle into infinity and back like a heartbeat. Blum Blom Blum Blom. . .

Here are some questions to practice with later. Come back and explore after you meet everyone here:
Does infinity have a middle?
Is infinity in each of us?
Is infinity in all of us?
Is infinity in both each of us and all of us?
Can infinity be outside of anything?
Can infinity be inside of anything?
What is an infinite feeling?
Is there a difference between a center and a middle?
Make up a question to explore.

With this simple motion you changed something with a simple rubber band! Imagine what you can do with your ideas, your intuition, and your imagination! Get ready to have fun with your imagination in The Land of Mystereum!

Remember that in the first chapter of each card there is a picture with a more general description that you can use to learn more about the card. It is not the only meaning. There are plenty more. It is where we begin that works best for us. We each evolve. In the second chapter of each card the real fun begins! The Mystereum Tarot card will speak directly to you. Each card has gifts for you that we call Imagination Tools. They are weightless. You can always have them whenever you need. Simply remember them. As you do, POOF, they are there for you!

Sometimes, simply feeling what you feel will be plenty with your ideas. Decide what feels right. Remember that we only ask two things of you here. First, look into each card's picture and tell yourself what comes to mind regardless of what the card tells you. Second, we ask that you practice with the Imagination Tools you receive. In time, we feel you will be a further whiz with your intuition and imagination! We look forward to the creative way that you put your gifts to wonderful use!

Enjoy doing Tarot readings with Mystereum's characters! Also, to fully experience your Imagination Primer feature, we suggest that you practice by doing Tarot readings where your readings are simply composed by the Imagination Tools each card you receive in your reading gifts you. Read your cards with your Imagination Tools as a Mystereum exercise. Apply the Imagination Tools AS your card indications utilizing the position in the Tarot spread each card you receive. Express your reading with only Imagination Tools as you actionably put them to good use, letting each Imagination Tool spark an action item for you to incorporate in your process.

Ready?
Enjoy The Land of Mystereum!
Have fun! ☺

Some Basic Ideas to Begin With ._._._._._._._._._._._._._._._.

All cards, both the Major Arcana and the Minor Arcana, come from experiences along The Fool's journey. These experiences are all inter-related and have been made into card characters. They nourish the journey with their unique and strong and distinct identities. The Minor Arcana have four suits: Pentacles, Cups, Wands, and Swords.

The Fool's eternal hope and optimism is always on the ready. This came from The Star card. You will see. The Temperance card brought The Fool to join the apparent opposites of above and below. There your material and spiritual qualities, your body and your mind, work together.

Sagittarius rules the Temperance card and is a wonderful expression of a uniquely complete being. Sagittarius is represented by a centaur. What is a centaur? A centaur is half man and half horse. It is a uniquely complete being. The centaur's tools are the bow and arrow. The bow is stationary. The arrow moves. They both work together to point the way like a compass. The bow and arrow and the centaur are not in union, though. Instead, we like to feel them like a family that work together.

To partner opposites is both the crux and a focus of a centaur to strengthen a uniquely complete identity. Chiron is the name of a really important centaur, a great healer. We were honored when he became Mystereum's mascot. When he became our mascot, he said, "Funny thing. You are each different, and you are each like everyone else." He laughed and laughed with a great smile. Continuing, he said, "The words for me as your mascot in Mystereum shall be, 'All similar, each unique. There is a wisdom when you are respectful and considerate and celebrate your ideas.'" He smiled and trotted off on his way. He lives in the night sky. He enjoys his constellation home in the stars. He asked us to mention that you look him up by simply looking up in the night sky. Each of his neighbors will twinkle or shine to you as you see them. He is up there in the sky hiding in plain sight to discover.

Part One

Archetypal Imagination

The Fool's Journey
Through the Major Arcana

Welcome to Mystereum's archetypes! We are the Major Arcana. We are here to show you the big picture in The Land of Mystereum! The Pentacles, Cups, Wands, and Swords form the Minor Arcana. They will show you a variety of places within The Land of Mystereum. The Fool will show up first. The Fool's identity is our avatar. Our avatar is the inner divinity we were born with. We feel it is the bright identity of our personality.

In Mystereum things are rarely equal. Everything is instead equally valuable. We believe there is a divinity present in each and every one of us. People, animals, concepts, and things. We feel it is our inner inheritance. We are each born with it. We have one overall dream. This dream is that our lives are exquisite experiences. We act with our imagination, our intuition, our creativity, and our ideas to keep this dream nourished and alive. Great timing! Here comes The Fool to meet you!

Ø The Fool ∞
Enter The Fool

I naturally express my place along the way of my journey. I experience grand exercises and powerful cycles. These experiences give me enthusiasm. I find and discover cool ideas and things. I also enjoy the scenery. My fave thing to be aware of is my feelings as I experience what is offered. I rarely know things. I act as I feel things in cycles and learn all the time. I know that it feels right, to feel right about how I feel and act, though. I use that along my way. My feelings are like a second heartbeat to me. I listen to them. They make great music for my journey.

When I meet someone, or encounter things along the way, I silently check my stomach for a second to see what it feels like to look in their eyes. I have heard that the soul speaks through the eyes. The eyes can tell you a lot. Remember, it is always your call here.

On my journeys I trust my feelings. I did not like or keep what I learned when I did not trust them. I remember so I do not repeat those times. In my experience . . . forgetting . . . is for getting. It makes more room to feel more good things. My feelings are not always comfortable, but they are mine. My many cycles of experience make vibrant travels.

The next people who will greet you are The Magician and The High Priestess. They taught me about the magic

The Fool
Journey, natural expressions, new directions

of things as they are. They are the ones who first thought up the rubber band game we put together for you. Like the rubber band game, my journey sometimes feels like a circle. Sometimes it feels like a branch. Sometimes it feels infinite. But, even when the rubber bands have fun being actors they are still rubber bands. I take that to heart. Sometimes they stretch!

The Magician is the one who told me that when I feel uncomfortable to do a gut-check and sense what my feelings tell me. Then, I choose to grow the way I do. Sometimes I feel afraid. At those times I pause and breathe and change my pace to rebalance myself. My fear usually tells me something important. Sometimes to duck! He taught me to realize that both have a different kind of gift for me. These gifts strengthen my choices. My previous experiences inform me. Even though I am always complete, I continue my journey. These gifts are one of the ways I keep my journey nourished with good things. I remember my past. But, I do not live there. The Magician taught me that my life has a special brand of magic. The High Priestess taught me not to let yesterday use up too much of today.

The Magician suggested I have a special respect for the ideas that influence me. "Keep the good ones," he said, "and squeeze and wring your sponge of the others. Stand under a waterfall in your mind while you visualize wringing your sponge when you need to." He is a lot of fun! He has this cool habit I call POOFIN'. All of a sudden and, POOF, he is right there! I still do not know how he does that. Pretty cool, though. I am learning.

I was really young when I first met THE MAGICIAN. I had just started to notice things around me. I began to explore. THE WORLD and THE WHEEL had come together so that I could be born and help you expand your imagination and enjoy your journey more. They taught me that I am both the origin of my journey and my journey itself. They taught me to feel my purest motives on my quests for discovery. I have felt things that worked great and those that. . . well, not so much at all. I remember those when similar things come up, but I depend more on my purest motives. I depend on the pure motives I like to be around. I remember how important it was when THE WORLD gave me free reign in this Land of Mystereum. The Kings do that now. THE WHEEL showed me how to sense and use patterns. They both asked me to remind myself of something whenever I felt perplexed or stuck. "Try a new perspective," they would say. "Try a new perspective. . .get back to YOURS!" ☺

Glad you could make it! I am here twinkle-fingering like a crab across the four, golden pillars of Mystereum. I call this golden symbol "Fabric." I found it in Mystereum long ago on my travels. I use this symbol to inform me how things work together. Use it when you please. It is called "Fabric."

I am THE FOOL and I LOVE to be on journeys. In fact I am always on a journey. I like it that way. Home is where my heart is. I love each card. They remind me further. Sometimes I like to pretend I am a circle. Sometimes I pretend I am the figure 8 on its side. All the while I am still always Me! I like pretend! If you ask me again tomorrow, I may tell you exactly the same thing. I may also tell you something different after I learn from a new experience. Sometimes my movements are bigger than at others. Sometimes they are teeny tiny.

If any of the Imagination Tools do not feel right for you, we all understand. We respect the emotional treasure of your honesty about what is right for you. Treasure is important to us. Things you feel are right and good and beneficial make us all smile and laugh and celebrate. You will see we like to celebrate a lot.

OH! Before The Mag does his cool POOFIN' thing, I want to give you another tip for your travels here. Ready? All of the Imagination Tools in The Land of Mystereum are weightless! Just remember them for a little bit, and they will be all warmed up and ready to use! WAIT! 1 2 3 4. You already know that!

Ready? Here are some Imagination Tools for you!

➣ IMAGINATION TOOLS FROM THE FOOL

- Feel and remember natural new directions you create as you move and evolve your ideas with imagination and creativity!

- Your imagination is a castle for your memories and ideas and dreams. Your imagination is all yours!

- Make yourself at home with your imagination. Keep it safe and warm. It is pricelessly valuable.

I The Magician

Think first spark, original idea, focus, and inception. This is NOT the Source of things, though. Here are your first inklings of your ideas and focus. These are inceptions. They are places to begin. This may be what you experience right before your rockin' first stroke over a blank page, right before you play that first electrifyin' sound!

THE MAGICIAN is like a bowl full of the night sky. He highlights the first sparks of your creations and your focus. His skills are his sense of humor, his wit, and his originality. He presents things clearly, but subtly distorted from the way you might expect. He creates new directions for you to take. He is the *arche* component of architecture. *Arche* means "to create." He is one who initiates and highlights ideas like shooting stars.

This is a card that flashes beginnings where your wits and strength come together. Notice the magic of your expectations. Notice the connections you make outside of expectations. Connections do not have to touch to be seamless. There is a magic in polarity that connects things to first-spark your ideas to cascade throughout your imagination.

THE MAGICIAN creates magical connections with things you have not seen. This helps uncover and clear out delusions and false starts. With a flap of his *eye*-wings he clears out unnecessary thoughts and ideas. As he does this, strengthen your focus. He suggests that you be serious and

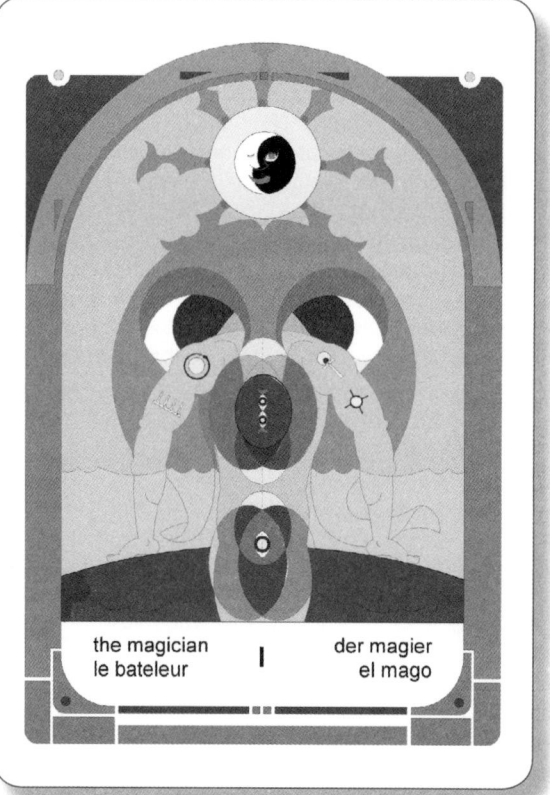

The Magician
First spark, focus, inception

playful at the same time. Keep misconceptions shaken off. Look at how you hold your mouth. Feel your posture. Let the expert skill of your imagination flow in your play.

When you feel those first sparks, the first inklings of the shooting stars of your ideas, remember them clearly and use them. Let the weather in your mind be natural to the way you feel. Keep the house of your creativity balanced. THE MAGICIAN's place has no clutter.

Imagine you are up on a hill over a beautiful lake. Enjoy the surroundings. Look way out in the center of the lake and see a clear glass of water just on top of the lake. Notice how still the water is. Then, (this part's really cool), calmly imagine a big rainstorm sweeping in. There is rain, and lots of thunder and lightning. Now, focus through the storm. Look through the storm to see your clear glass of water untouched by the storm. The top of the water untouched by the rain and wind. Your clear glass of water is completely still. Sense the storm all around but focus on this clear and still water in the middle of it all. There is another tool!

Your calm and clear glass of water in the middle of this storm is your insight that lives in a pure vessel. It is there all the time when you need it. Focus like the bird called an Ibis that stands over the water looking down at a fish. If you reach for where you see the fish, you will miss it. Water does this wonderful thing that distorts perception. It is called refraction. But, the Ibis feels the fish more than simply seeing it. The Ibis can reach across worlds from air to under the water to the fish. The Ibis does not reach to the place where it sees the fish. It reaches to the place where the fish actually *is*. THE MAGICIAN and Ibis help your aim.

Remember the Ibis looking into the water as you look into any rainstorm. Find your calm glass of water. See where it is? Either way, feel where it is! Put the Ibis and your glass of water together as two magical eye-wings, two ends of a living magic wand. One wing feels below. The other feels above. THE MAGICIAN has an intense focus to direct his vibrant enthusiasm as he flaps the wand of his living eye-wings!

Enter The Magician

POOF! Thanks for bringing me to appear for you! Thank You! You did that when you came to this page! I am THE MAGICIAN. My favorite animal is the Ibis. The Ibis is a really neat bird that has an amazing skill to focus its energies. It has extremely sharp, vibrant, and dynamic vision. It can aim at things underwater even though locations are distorted from what it sees from above. I also love vessels and houses and places where great things begin. I love spaces where great things are placed. I love twilight as I begin to feel my own light in the dark each night.

I love it when the first spark of an idea zips though my weightless sky like a shooting star. I look at things in different ways. Original ideas are like magical stars shooting across my night sky. You see I am like a bowl of night sky in your imagination. I am uncluttered. I am the natural home for your clear mind where ideas are born and roam free. The Greeks called me *Arche*. *Arche* is the first part of the word "architecture." It means the place of the original idea or its inception. It means "to create."

What do you see here in my picture? How does that make you feel? Pretend now as you flap the living wand of your magical eye-wings. Pretend to put what you see and feel together. Smile big as you say what it is out loud or to yourself. POOF! I am still here. That was YOU! You put things together in your imagination for real! Smile it again!

So, let me introduce you to some more Imagination Tools.

➤ IMAGINATION TOOLS
FROM THE MAGICIAN

- Construct a house of creativity for your imagination in your mind.

- See and feel your clear and still glass of water on the lake. Feel this as your insight that lives in a pure vessel. It is there any time you need it. If you cannot see it, close your eyes and feel for it. Breathe deeply and you will feel it appear.

- When your magic feels missing, look into your blind spots. Look into the things you expect to see. Then flap your wings and move what is actually there.

My ideas-into-action counterpart is waiting to meet you. She is not very excitable. Her work is quite huge. She took the Ibis-eyed focus of my magical eye-wings and spread them through her whole being. It is in every ounce of her presence, and she made it all her own. She takes these formless ideas I have and gives them form. It excites me that she has her own magic! Enjoy meeting THE HIGH PRIESTESS!

II The High Priestess

Think intuition and inner illumination. Think conception from first spark. THE HIGH PRIESTESS is the character of your hidden influences at work. Unrevealed futures unfold here. She works with the creature forces of your unconscious. She contemplates their meditations as she meditates their contemplations all at one time.

She gives form to ideas. She makes them real. THE MAGICIAN highlighted the initial spark of creation with the bowl of his night sky. THE HIGH PRIESTESS conceives and forms an idea from that spark. THE MAGICIAN aims through distortions. THE HIGH PRIESTESS clearly transforms this aim. Formlessness is given form here. She is the *techne* component of the word "architecture." THE MAGICIAN creates. THE HIGH PRIESTESS makes and gifts form to ideas. She puts ideas together. *Techne* means "to put together, to make."

She hears most worries as echoes of previous, unresolved expectations. She lets them pass as she focuses her senses. Feel what is really present as you practice and make the best course for your ideas. Take care if you worry. Ibis-eye the worry. Look to THE MAGICIAN as you feel your ideas. Look to THE EMPRESS who comes next to begin to bring them to full term. Here, though, focus with THE HIGH PRIESTESS to give form to your ideas!

THE HIGH PRIESTESS suggests to have the utmost patience with your ideas. Be in sync with what you make manifest.

The High Priestess
Intuition, forming, conception

Harness your passions. Be mindful of them. Outline priorities and give form to your ideas. She suggests that this is a time to orchestrate your momentum rather than going full speed. Use your presence here.

She has a powerful and thorough process. Her work is continuous. She also stays rested. She works like your body grows. Use her direct intuition and her process. It is powerful. Her ways help you give form to your ideas. Use your presence.

Enter The High Priestess

I am the other half of architecture with THE MAGICIAN. As you are aware the Greeks called THE MAGICIAN's work the *Arche*. He starts ideas. I make and put them together. The Greeks called my work *techne*. I put things together. I make. Discipline of the ritual is my common thread. My method when I want to form things is to stand at my easel, or to sit in my chair, or put myself in the place where my tools and materials are located. It is that simple. "Butt in the chair," I say. What comes from that is different each time. My pace and rhythm are important. I never hurry even when I am moving fast. I am also not resting when I move more slowly. I move in accord with my work. Your imagination forms the pace of how I work. Your ideas play with its rhythm.

I flow in right after that first spark across the house of your creativity to begin to give form to your ideas. I am often hidden. I also leave no trace. I work very cleanly across everything on the table or easel or floor or wherever I work. I build unrevealed futures so that the next character you meet here can carry them to full term. She is a 3, the first number of composition and beauty. I, as THE HIGH PRIESTESS, am a 2. I bring things together. THE MAGICIAN is a 1. He is a place to begin. I am a place that forms. Remember that The Mag is the place of the start of an idea. He may not be the first thing to happen.

I ask that you have the utmost respect for your ideas. I do. You can relax here and watch for now if you want as my home is a very expansive place. I am here to encourage your ideas while you develop your imagination and creativity further. We have made this Land of Mystereum so that you can make it yours.

Sometimes I am the night sky in your mind. There I am darkness that is lush and not to be feared. I am honored to have welcomed you here. I raise my hands with the utmost respect for your imagination. I would like you to breathe deeply as I present your gift. The gift I bestow to you is the form of The Land of Mystereum for you to use when you are ready. Imagine it like in a time before there was a map. I give you a place for your imagination to roam free and form ideas as you please.

As you gaze into my picture bring one of your ideas to mind as you remember your clear and still glass of water.

We dedicate this land to your imagination. We encourage you to use it as often as you please. Bring an idea to mind as you breathe. Close your eyes and nod when you are ready to move on.

In all reverence to the light of your imagination, I bid you farewell for now. I disappear into the moon as I say, "Namaste, from my light to yours. From my light to yours."

☞ *IMAGINATION TOOL* FROM THE HIGH PRIESTESS

- The Land of Mystereum is for you to use with your imagination to form your ideas. Share your imaginative form with your friends here and there. Do so in ways that are right for you that shine forth your best qualities. Be considerate of others' light. May all your lights form well together and shine like stars.

III The Empress

THE EMPRESS carries the form of ideas to full term. While THE MAGICIAN feels the primal spark or inception of an idea, creates it, and THE HIGH PRIESTESS gives the idea form, conceives it and makes it, THE EMPRESS carries the idea to full term. THE EMPRESS gives ideas life!

This card indicates abundance, sensuality, and gifts of the earth in regard to your focus. Notice the "embrace your earthly desires" quality of THE DEVIL card that comes later. THE EMPRESS provides a balance that lives in a lush yet mundane place. Strong and new enthusiasm is here. Enjoy your ideas as if for the first time. Let their inter-relationships begin as they are born.

Fully formed ideas come to life here between these trees in The Land of Mystereum. These trees provide shelter and establish a place for things to come to life. Think of your character here. You. Think and feel. What part do you play? THE FOOL lets you be anything. You can be anything you want here, too. Think and feel exactly what it is that you are. It can change over time. Do not let your answer, or no answer, worry you. Simply enjoy thoughts that rise at twilight or dawn. Think of what you want to do with them. Maybe you want to play a little here before you decide. Feel free. Take the opportunity. Establish your character more fully. Pretend a little. Think about it. Feel into it.

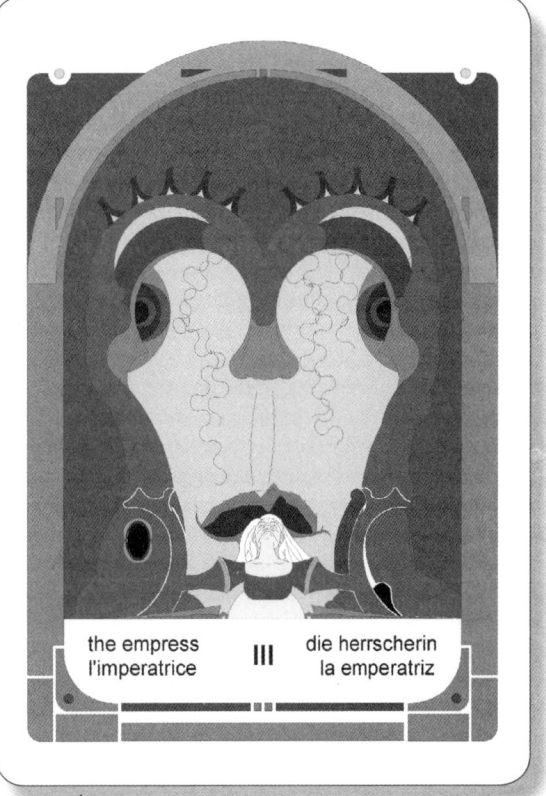

The Empress
Fresh, nurturing, bringing to life

Enter The Empress

Pause and look into my picture as you let your imagination roam. If you can smile when you feel what you just felt, you may be ready to say it. I do not rush things. Life is sacred to me that way. Take your time. Look into my picture. These trees are very old. Close your eyes and look around them. Remember that it is your call here. When you are ready say, "I am going to _____!" Say it with gusto! I would like all of my gardens in Mystereum to hear it! Make it more fun that way. Make it more ALIVE! Sing it to the treetops!

Now, feel how stable your character is when you smile with bright eyes. What are your favorite ways to balance and move? We will add some crucial final touches. These will happen over time. Your character is now alive in the story! What does your real-time pretend character you look like? I smile and hope your character looks a lot like you. Costumes are fun, too!

Now that I have had the honor to meet you, I would like to give you your treasure from this part of Mystereum. Before I do, I would like you to close your eyes and remember this: In The Land of Mystereum and your imagination, you are the boss. As you learn and grow, you will experience things. Old things. New things. You will experience things that enhance you. Things that will change you. Things that will reinforce you. Things that will strengthen you. You will also enhance things with your influence. Make things more full with a smile and life while you do. Reinforce and strengthen your ideas. I find this to be normal, and also pretty cool!

Sometimes you change things when you simply strengthen yourself. You are strong and aware. Keep sight of that, Dearheart. Now please slowly open your eyes.

Hello there, Dearheart. I am THE EMPRESS. I smile and welcome you to another place on your journey of exploration and discovery. Some people tell me I am wise, but I feel I simply mirror the Earth. Everything given form and conceived by THE HIGH PRIESTESS is brought to full term here. Smile at her golden glow towards the bottom of my picture. Her golden glow is pregnant with form to carry ideas to full term. Bring ideas to life right here under the canopy of my tree-cheeks. See! My eyes are up in the tree under my crazy hair. Take a look around my picture. See what you see. Remember that idea THE HIGH PRIESTESS had you bring to mind.

I am THE EMPRESS and I love to carry ideas to full term. My treasure from under my Empress Trees is the golden glow when I see you bring your ideas to full term in your imagination and you give them life. Sometimes you will know. Sometimes you will be comfortable with the *not-knowing*. Feel how best to respect your ideas as you bring them to life. Enjoy the treasure of a golden glow as you bring your ideas to life!

↠ *Imagination Tool*
From The Empress

- I give you a golden glow as your bring your ideas to life. Crayons are a great way to begin using your new Imagination Tool!

Tell my son, The Hanged Man, hello with love when you meet him. His heart grew from these trees when he followed it.

IV The Emperor

The Emperor is the overseer of Mystereum's external world and order. Here, "A" leads to "B" leads to "C" with thoughtful logic. By going step by step, in a single step, even in surprise, The Emperor can re-align the pace of the whole system when he responds. The Emperor indicates that you can be a strong role model. You can establish flexible boundaries for the vested interests of your ideas. Your ideas are your creative subjects. They live in your imagination.

Take in all of these surroundings. Your inner world can be very connected to your outer world here. All is seen clearly in the fresh, new place The Emperor makes for your new and alive ideas. The Emperor suggests not to act untrue to your ideas. Look to this place where you can take them step by step. Look to The Empress for the life you begin with your ideas. Look forward to The Hierophant for the overall feel of your ideas as you begin to think of homes for your ideas. Take them step by step here.

Enter The Emperor

Hello and welcome! I see you have found your way here to this magical inside-outside place. My chief talent is to order places in Mystereum. Order up! I keep to the bargains I make, and leave room for improvement as they evolve.

The Emperor
Overseer, place-maker, methodical

My Empress lends her vibrant gardens and trees so I may develop safe places for you to explore your imaginings. I am THE EMPEROR. My main concern in life is a sense of place. I bring order to places. First, I feel the order in my imagination. Then, I consult with my Empress about how best to bring this order to full term. Then, with the wave of my hand, I honor great ideas as I work with them. This way my developments incorporate the order created by ideas to make place.

I would like to express that I feel you have an imaginative power and an ability to see the big picture. JUSTICE and STRENGTH will increase your field of vision soon enough. For now, start with the big picture. That is here in my character. It is a natural order. Feel your imaginative power and all the things around you. Let us walk this place a bit together, shall we?

Look in to my picture. See how my horse helps? Those people by the campfire are some of my most trusted ideas. I wanted to revel in their grand interactions with no interference. This way I can decide to build new places as they grow and evolve. My horse whinnied to me that she would slip in, lie down, and turn into a tree to mask me. She settled into the ground at a distance from them. Her ideas help me to establish the form and character of this place without interference. Some things I leave natural. Some things I change outright. I love a natural sense of order.

As THE EMPEROR, I love being the overseer. I love going step by step. In any single step along the way, even in surprise, I can re-align my pace and direction to keep our natural order fresh. The interaction of my ideas helps me to plan and explore with deliberate action. They make me so proud! They also go step by step. They are really the genius of my place here. I am a simple man when you come down to it. My gift to you is no less simple. In your imagination please be attentive to your placements. Have a patient presence with your placements. Your natural sense of order builds foundations under your dreams. The way you place your ideas forms a natural order to build your dreams.

Enjoy your placement even when it challenges you! If you begin to feel depleted, it may be due to misspent efforts. Keep a close eye on your actions without worry. Keep a far one, too, as you pay attention. With practice you will learn to do these together.

⇒ IMAGINATION TOOLS
FROM THE EMPEROR

- I give you the gift to notice and develop your own natural *sense of order*. Feel the presence of your imagination as an idea solar system. Each idea can orbit like a planet or moon. Stars, comets, and asteroids can also orbit. Practice with your placements and how you orbit your ideas. Cycles await you to strengthen your ability to be counted upon and to be reasonable. Feel the value of where you place your ideas.

- There is a great deal in the small gift above. To create an additional Imagination Tool I encourage you to *see* and *feel* each of the first gift's parts one by one as a puzzle. Put them together in your own way!

V The Hierophant

THE HIEROPHANT indicates a tradition that is *wise* and soothes. He brings spiritual qualities to the earth and to your divine *mindbodybeautiful*. Make a temple of your body. Make a resting place for your soul. Make a seat for your mind. Here life itself, from beginning to end, inspires each moment. Your spirit is brought to join with your body on earth at birth. This continues through life. It especially continues here!

THE HIEROPHANT leans back to drive the universe on cruise control. This can infuse new spirit into your ideas. Your ideas and your story are in and around you. Picture your Source here. Picture what is so big and so *there* you cannot *see* it. Visualize where you began. See where you will go. Feel the spirit of your ideas here!

Enter The Hierophant

I am the source of your life force. I fill you with light. I permeate Mystereum along with THE HERMIT. His wise and reflective light comes to provide a darkness that consolidates ideas like the moon. Through the wisdom of that which is pure and *not-knowing*, I provide an inner light which turns on the mystery of life itself. Turn on the mystery of life itself within you! Feel it in ideas!

The Hierophant
Wisdom, new spirit, activation

I smile to infuse your mind and body with spirit, a *mindbodybeautiful* that is all your own. Close your eyes and bring your dreams and ideas into view. Remember your cup of still water. Remember THE MAGICIAN's bowl of night sky. I bring your dreams down to earth. Your spirit brightens them. I ask you to meet up with me and bring your dreams and ideas to reality from within!

I ask you to enhance the meaningful things in your life. Win, lose, or draw, 100 percent. Remember that. No matter what, 100 percent, I root for YOU! I ask you to be aware of bad-coach math. Never give your 110 percent. Never. You will overextend yourself. But, when they say that, smile and give it your ALL! They simply ask you to excel and grow to a new 100 percent. Excel with your 100 percent to brighten your inner light and strengthen and fill a greater 100 percent.

My gift of inner light sits with your gift of inner light. I welcome you to this place that permeates all of Mystereum. I welcome you to the place of the Mystereum spirit. I welcome you to feelings and ideas that are infused to support your imagination. I welcome the inner light of your ideas. I welcome you here. Welcome!

I bring spiritual things to the earth. What I love most is that you can be like a temple or church. Your parents made you, and YOU infuse your spirit into your place. You light up your mind. You enliven your body. You are beautiful! Love that.

I am THE HIEROPHANT. I love to be a *mindbodybeautiful* connection to your natural divinity. To me *mindbodybeautiful* is all one word. Like a temple or church that is built, feel the spirit of your *mindbodybeautiful*.

My lesson is all about the gift that is your inner strength! Please accept my seated posture to give you the power to keep your imagination strong. Fill it with spirit. I ask only that you grow your spirit from the inside. Grow from your core as you work with others. Please accept my seated posture. I sit here for you with all of your ideas to provide a seat for your mind. I say, "Namaste." Nom-a-stay. I gift you a seat for your mind.

➤ *Imagination Tools* From The Hierophant

- I give to you the ability to sit with strength. Know that to acknowledge someone is a great compliment.
- I ask that you first acknowledge yourself as you sit. Sit out to the universe. It is there for you.
- I gift you a seat for your mind. May you feel its spirit and fill it with love.

VI The Lovers

Imagine a cross-roads filled with vibrant energy, confidence, and purpose. Mutual respect is wholeheartedly felt and embraced. Love is indicated as the ultimate, reciprocal respect and embrace of one identity for another. This is a person, a spirit, a place, a thing [okay, a noun ☺]. Here is a honored quality to join with another as you provide powerful witness to who they are from their perspective in a way that catalyzes you both. There is an "Is-ness" to nearness in this pair, this joinery. Vibrant joinery creates more. The Lovers' identities are intact. They are as two seraphims that call to one another.

The Lovers enhance all of the characteristics of themselves and those in orbit around them. Are respect and love different? The Gemini twins of The Lovers express love taken to a higher level. They express a galactic center level of love as they cycle through orbits where mundane things are not less. This is the card of the joining.

Note, too, the sequence of The Lovers. They come after The Hierophant infuses divinity within. They come before The Chariot's powerful and invigorated harmony of opposites. Note the vibrancy of energies in the joinery of them both here. Look what they do with the symbol of Fabric.

Enter The Lovers

We smile to you! We join and harmonize as two distinct lives or ideas. THE CHARIOT will harmonize passionate and seemingly disparate energies. We suggest that you look to THE HIEROPHANT to fuel your life force. Then, feel us. Look to THE CHARIOT as you direct your passions. Then, look back to us. We iron out misperceptions as we join things together.

We would like to show you vibrant joineries in the harmony of all that is you! We bring lovers and ideas and compatible energies together to enhance the freedom of both. Our strength together eliminates the need for worry. We ask you to feel the vibrancy of your confidence and purpose. Feel the strength of wholehearted self-respect in the powerful experience of love for yourself while you love your ideas! We do!

We offer you a vitality at every scale here! If you ever feel you have lost that, simply pause and smile as you remember us. Your smile calls us. We offer you wholehearted presence. We simply ask that you do not avoid fears, and be aware of falling and loud noises. Are there any other innate fears that are worthwhile? Are those even? Falling and loud noises may not be the only two, but we have not found any others worth much consideration. In fact, after much time and attentive conversation with each other, the loud noises are simply loud. They do not startle us much anymore. We simply respond, or smile a pause into our conversation. We sometimes find good things when we fall. It can add a different perspective.

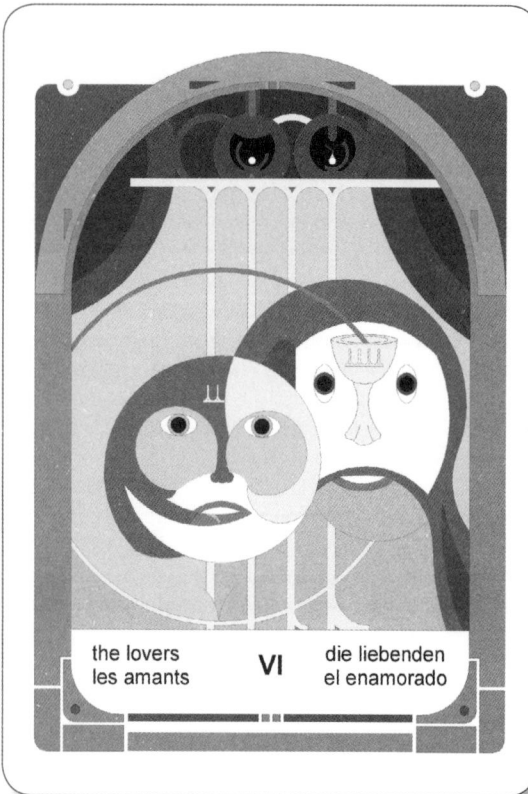

The Lovers
Vitality, reciprocation, powerful witness

We suggest that you breathe consciously for two minutes if worries appear. Make worries work for it. Do not let worries erode your progress. We have not found many worries that ever lasted longer than two minutes. They are usually *zzzzz*'ing by about just over twenty seconds of conscious breathing. Look up narcissism. They may live there. Let them. We do not invite them here. If they show up unannounced, we work together to flip 'em with our united front! We do not waste worry. We also work to keep its vines out of the things we join.

We are everything that you bring together. We welcome you to our neck of the woods! We do not have union. We enhance and strengthen our identities and our priorities together. We feel that union often makes an average of things that does not last very long. But, OH do we blend and influence each other! We listen to each other with powerful witness. Our embrace is as strong as life itself!

We love vibrancy, healthy energies, happy confidence, focused purpose, and wholehearted respect that is felt and embraced.

We love. And, we love what we love!

We love vibrant joineries in mutual harmony.

We would like you to feel the places that you make strong partnerships with your ideas. In the sandbox. At play. With your friends. Smile fully in these rockin' places! They often show you the way forward into new things, and refresh the ones you have.

⇒ *IMAGINATION TOOL*
FROM THE LOVERS

- We ask you to see vibrant partnerships. Bow in respect as you embrace them. Form them further with your bow of strength as you point them together with the arrow of your actions.

- We also would simply like to say something. We feel that you are always a part of your agreements. Make them with heart.

VII The Chariot

THE CHARIOT brings powerfully different, inner forces into harmony. Agility in the speed and power of your process is indicated. Take note of your strategies as chariots typically engage from the side. Look to the powerful forces in your life to feel where any strain needs to be tuned back in to balance. This tuning is crucial. The embodiment of stand-alone, self-nourishing connections is present in the agility of your actions.

WOW! A powerfully invigorated union of opposites that pulls different directions is in harmony here! The mix may feel frenetic at first until you acclimate. You succeed here by calmly directing your ideas and engaging them with passion at speed from the side. They ride with you, alongside you, and within you! Bring the powerfully different, inner forces of your ideas into harmony here.

Enter The Chariot

I am often depicted with two sphinx. Here, I have two horses. My chariot is stationary as the Centaur's bow. The arrow of each of my horses has an active, inner direction. They are both wildly passionate and driven. Without harmony these two horses would snap the bow of my chariot and tear it apart.

The Chariot
Harmony, agility, speed

Look to the powerful forces in your life to feel where strain needs to be tuned. There is indication here to take decisive action to rectify any discord. Think of music. Listen to music that moves you. Listen to the individual instruments and sounds coming together. Hear your favorite music inside and tune your accents and solos.

All cards can stand alone as a place unto themselves. But, I am the embodiment of stand-alone, self-nourishing connections. I am life in motion in the universe. We charioteers move in headlong with full force and then engage from the side. Ours is a strategy to be wise in time and act in the moment.

OH! This is my personal fave Chariot Idea! Visualize yourself in a vast field of sunflowers bursting with their gold petals and brown centers! Vibrant contrasts grow and glow together! Feel around. Focus on one sunflower. Feel the brilliant contrast of the brown center with the gold petals. Green stalks support the flower and connect to the brown earth. The earth below is connected to the brown in the middle by strong, green stalks. The sun above shines on the vibrant gold petals. The sky touches the gold petals of your ideas and the sun and beyond! Feel the vibrancy of above and below in the sunflower!

I am all about balance! I have to be! My high performance movements are quick and sure. You see, I am a CHARIOTEER! My vehicle only works well at speed. Powerfully different things work together in balance as I direct my horses to draw me forward with VROOMMMMM! I love powerful, invigorated things that pull in different directions that I harness together in harmony.

Do you like music? I like lots of notes put together that make wonderful music that moves me! I love music and voices and ideas that give me the tingles.

I would like you to see you drive a chariot entirely your own in your imagination. Feel how your feet touch the floor. Feel how you can shift your weight to move it different directions with your feet. Your toes can be little ground-grabbers, like fingers for your feet. I find it is often a light touch that steers the best. It is a strong touch, a very direct feeling. But, it is subtle.

And, that is where I will like to let you in on my secret. I do not worry about missing my target when I am aiming for something. Remember the Ibis. Speed does that water distortion thing to your aim. My secret is my strategy. I move my chariot in from the side to match up and mesh with the object of my focus. This way I can accurately match and connect with my aim. I control nothing. I engage in sync. My natural agility with ideas at speed then gets the job done!

I would like to give you agility in how you respond to things! I would like to give you strategy to place your agility. I suggest that this is a great time to feel the agility in your responsiveness! Next you will meet the heartbeat of how I harmonize things so well. Justice. I suggest that you not distract yourself with that now. Feel how you sync up with your ideas and respond to them in action at speed.

⇒ *Imagination Tools*
From The Chariot

- I give to you the strategy of syncing up with ideas so you can respond with more ease in motion. I give you strategy that is as agile as a powerful smile!

- Visualize yourself in a vast field of sunflowers that burst forth with their gold petals and brown centers on a sunny day with a clear sky! The earth is below. The sun is above. The sunflower reaches to the ground as the gold petals of your ideas touch the sun and beyond! Feel this Chariot Idea permeate you as you imagine a vast field of brilliant sunflowers! Each may be an idea!

- I gift you full-on strong YAH breathing to aspirate your ideas with high performance!

VIII Justice

Justice indicates that your life and ideas are in balance. You are strong because you are fair. Your wisdom is that you are considerate. You are honest with what you see and feel is present. Be considerate of yourself and how you balance your ideas. Justice is the card of ultimate fairness. It is not coercive or persuasive. Justice is never punitive. Be mindful of its honesty. At times its honesty may feel brutal. With creativity, though, there is no right or wrong here. There are simply consequences. Weigh the consequences of your ideas in balance honestly. Prune, adjust, and change as you weigh them if you need.

Be mindful of different affects that the same action will have on each and every thing in your idea solar system. Do not focus too much on the good or bad in your ideas or others' ideas. That opens you up to the potential of punitive or malicious actions. Simply be mindful of your ideas as you balance them. Be mindful of others just as they are. Rather than respectful or non-judgmental, be "considerate." Unique identities and personalities have their own places. You will find them here in balance.

An inner scale is indicated by Justice to weigh your decisions and guide the patterns you form. Your mental and physical well-being and that of any system in which you are involved needs to be seen with an eye to health that is wholly

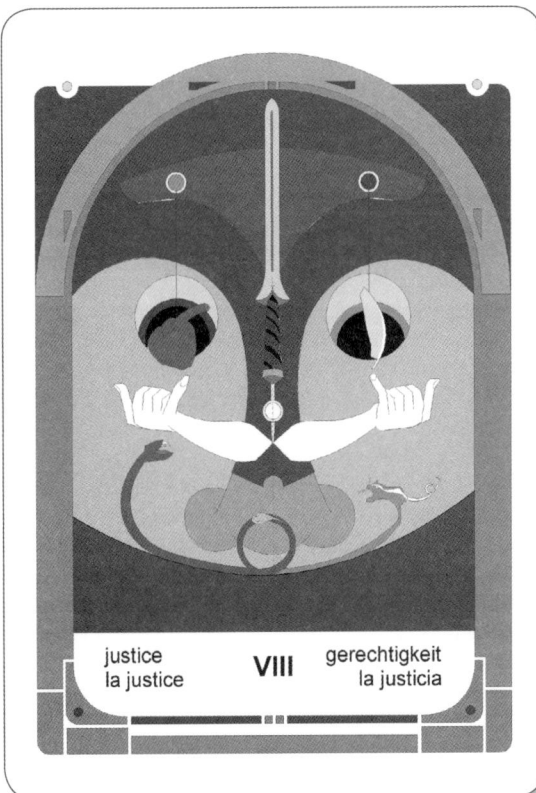

Justice
Balance, befitting, honest

appropriate to it rather than imposed on it. Do not contrive things. Do not force things. Simply ask yourself if the health of the personality of an idea or person is positive for you. No judgment on them. If they are positive for you, it usually feels like a good idea to play and learn with them.

Enter Justice

Be mindful of any imbalance or misplaced efforts in your scene. Look to THE CHARIOT to discern the harmony of the forces in play. Look to the darkness of THE HERMIT who comes next to consolidate your clarity. You will know to proceed when you feel and balance them both together with your ideas. My place is to welcome all of your imagination. Any time you feel out of balance you have a place to tune yourself up. Take a break to let something settle if you feel overwhelmed. Be fair to yourself and visit here to balance and tune your ideas.

My place in Mystereum is one to forget your expectations and feel how things actually are. I am a place to get to the present reality of your situation. This is a great place to come and find your own perspective when you are perplexed or feel blocked. There are lots of different scales to work with here.

Ginormous ones. Huge ones. Large ones. Medium ones. Small ones. And, there are teeny, tiny ones, too. Some of them may be so big and so *there* you do not see them. Some of them are so small that they may seem invisible.

For your first exercise here, I encourage you to shift your focus as you redirect yourself between these scales. Use the scales in fairness. Do not concentrate on right or wrong. Simply focus on the consequences of the things you weigh. Worry is not allowed in JUSTICE. Consequences and outcomes are important here. They are always just as they are as they inform your imagination.

If you do not like an outcome, please feel free to act differently the next time. Weigh other values so your feelings come across just right the next time. You will get it. I would like to suggest that you not be judgmental or even non-judgmental of people or yourself. Be considerate. Your ideas have value. Values that you weigh will help you make decisions. I propose that this first exercise with your scales is to simply be considerate of yourself. Others need not be agreeable. See how you weigh in for you as you practice here. Consideration fits my energies. There is JUSTICE with the values that I hold.

Be mindful of yourself just as you are. Be mindful of others just as they are. I would like you to weigh these things for yourself. Always feel free to discuss values with people close to you. Make yourself at home here. These are your scales.

Now that THE CHARIOT has shown you enlivened things at speed, I will show you something special about your imaginative activity. Your imagination is constantly dreaming and informs your heart. As JUSTICE I do not put forth a right or a wrong. I am about accurate and aware creativity. Here, creativity is simply about the accuracy with which you weigh your feelings about your ideas, the choices you then make with actions, and the consequences those actions make for your ideas.

I am JUSTICE. I love to bring life back into balance with a strong and valuable fairness. I do not choose sides. I simply weigh the values across the whole.

Remember my suggestion of that first exercise to try. Weigh being considerate of yourself and others without simply being agreeable. If you have already done that, please feel free to settle in here and do it again before you move on. There are some very active characters coming up soon. I want you to be comfortable when you weigh situations as you meet them. This takes practice. I feel you will get more out of your Imagination Tools if you work here with me a bit. You may begin to give yourself some tools that are all your own, too. Remember that you matter. You are valuable.

My gift for your imagination is a magical inner scale of weights and measures. It is magic simply by imagining it to be so. The size of your scales will change as you imagine them to do so. You can even imagine this magical scale to be two or more scales. You can imagine it to be of different shapes and sizes. This inner scale is also weightless so it fits in your imagination with no effort. It is weightless like a memory or a dream. You can take it anywhere. It will always be ready for you to use. Imagine yourself right back here if you ever need quiet. I recommend that you practice with your new and magical inner scale. Get used to how it works for you. Get comfortable with how you move and weigh value with it.

⇒ *Imagination Tools*
From Justice

- I give to you a magical inner scale of weights and measures to help you weigh things while you experience them. It can be made to any size. Simply imagine it to be so and it will POOF to your exact needs.

- I give you a love of a balanced imaginative life. May it be strong and fair and without gimmicks. May it do what is necessary to balance your feelings in equilibrium.

IX The Hermit

The Hermit indicates your inner activity and the clarity you see in mysteries and things that seem to lack form in darkness. His experience is similar to a walk through your mind as a walk around a cloister. You may be acutely aware of completed cycles of your experiences. Focus on these clearly. Meditate on them from within. The Hermit provides a time and place to be active inside. Others may not see what you see or feel what you see and feel.

The Hermit is not stationary. He is both bow and arrow as one. With this thought, do not maintain or hold static perspectives. Now is a poignant time to sense YOUR perspective and believe in what you feel.

The Hermit indicates a clarity of vision into mysteries. Think enlightenment. Think inner illumination. The Hermit encourages long walks. Listen to the sounds that your feet make as you walk. Be silently aware of where they are.

A feeling of consolidation where things come together is also indicated as you are aware and see your own footprints in a new place. Your perspective can refresh a place that you have already been to as you experience it in a different light. Though peace and solitude are also indicated, a closer look may reveal a light inside you that is very active and bright. Think of a lantern viewed up close. Clarity is indicated to be present regardless of outside influences. Clarity is present and felt brightly

The Hermit
Inner light, perspective, silent awareness

Enter The Hermit

Shine a light on your mysteries and confusion. Turn over the pretty rocks of your beliefs. Discover as you reveal. I am never stationary. I am always on the move whether on foot or in my mind. Use your own long, mind-whiskers to feel the wisdom of your way. My way is not reclusive. My way is active and mindful inside. I ask that you be patient with your insights. Others may not see or feel what you see and feel. I suggest that any anger you feel is a simple indication of misunderstandings. Do not be misunderstood. Engage your clarity and bring any misunderstandings to light.

Sense your perspective as you experience it. I gather that your perspective is specific, and also not static. Visualize a bow and arrow as one identity. That is my wisdom. That is my way. It moves me. Sense your perspective. If you are grumpy, take a walk. If you are peaceful, light a special candle and keep it near.

I love the clarity of vision that comes from the breadth of my experiences. You see, I see into mysteries and confusion as clearly as I notice my footsteps and complete my cycles, my circles. Many times the scenery would never clue me in to this. But, as I see my footsteps, I remember that I have been here before. I remember the place as it was. I sense OH BOY how different it is NOW! And, I continue to explore. I am as clear as my footsteps.

If you see me in one spot for a great amount of time, do not worry. I do not stagnate. Do not feel that I am stationary, either, even when I am still. Relish that I love to walk the cloister of my mind. You can do this, too. Your land might be bigger than Mystereum. Watch your steps. Notice them. See them clearly. Explore them as you explore with them. Remember the places you would like to come back to over time. They will change as much as you do as time goes on. I often stop and relish in the newfound glories I find in a very familiar place. We can keep each other fresh and mobile here, inside and out. THE CHARIOT will help us get places quickly. And, as you walk in your mind, I will show you how to keep mystery fresh while you further discover things. I complete cycles. I smile inside as I think about what rolls around next.

I love my lantern. It is a symbol of my inner light unmoved by outside influences.

⇒ IMAGINATION TOOLS
FROM THE HERMIT

- I give to you the idea of a magical cloister as your imagination for long walks. Venture to explore and discover and feel the treasure of your patterns and cycles.
- I give you fresh mysteries to unfold.
- I present you with an inner lantern for clarity.

I was just thinking. Thought you might enjoy this. A cloister has a garden. The garden has a hallway around it. The hallway has columns that are open to the garden. The garden is open to the sky. The hallway is under a roof. The garden is open air under the roof of the sky. The whole cloister is within a building.

I feel that the cloister is much like your imagination. Your body and mind can be the hallway and building around it as you see the sky from the garden in your imagination. The open roof in the cloister is much like your eyes. May they sparkle as they shine from the inner cloister of your imagination.

Also, the ancient Greeks often built their homes with a courtyard in the middle that was open to the sky. You can also think of this type of house along with your cloister. Enjoy the interesting history of the places you associate with, discover, and make.

Here is an exercise for you. I request that you imagine earth, wood, fire, water, and metal in a garden. Make sure you are safe and do no harm to you or others. You can visualize a candle, a lantern, or even a flashlight for fire. Do not leave fire unattended. Be creative. See how you feel they grow. I call this my Cloister Seed. Water it with your imagination and breath. Light it with your eyes. A whole world can exist in the tiniest of things and the smallest of places.

X The Wheel

THE WHEEL indicates that all luck on this day is yours. Look down. Is there something valuable to find? Big things are here. There is luck and change. There is fortune, abundance, and happiness. Think of what THE HERMIT expressed to you. Sense your return to places that you now see in a different way. Feel completions in play.

THE WHEEL, or THE WHEEL OF FORTUNE, indicates that you have just won or are about to win a figurative lottery, of which there are many types. Sense your imagination and inner inheritances as your ideas become like a lottery you have just won. Your wishes are indicated to come true out of the blue. This may be with a special person or a sought after project or job. You may receive a reward for your hard work. You may get that break that you have been looking for. Here is change in a way that almost always brings joy along with it.

Enjoy your luck and ideas in a big way. Place yourself where you want to be and flow naturally. Enjoyment is yours. Feel your natural placement. When you work, think only of the work you do. You have taken the next step past THE HERMIT. You have a complete cycle. Enjoy things in a wonderful variety of ways here.

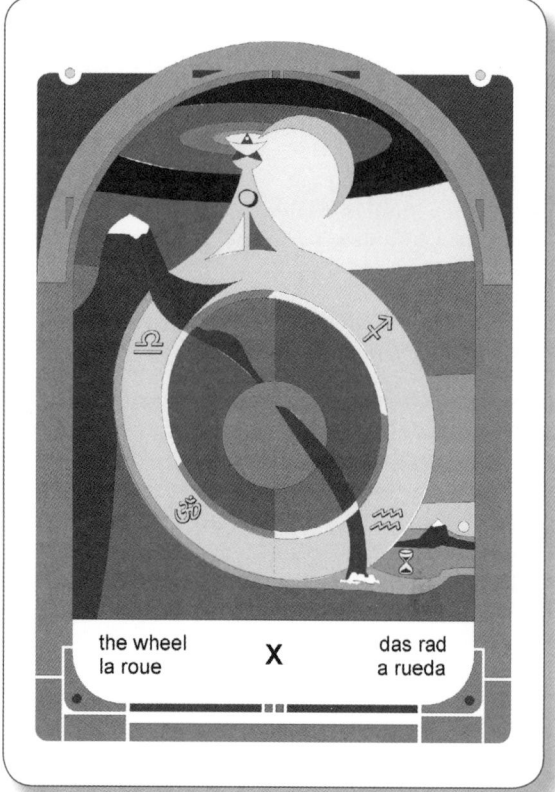

The Wheel
Cycles, orbits, luck

Enter The Wheel

As THE WHEEL OF FORTUNE I indicate big things to you. I express your luck and your changes. I show you the vibrant fortune of your inner inheritances. JUSTICE gave you a magical scale. There is a place of your choice here to play with that. Anywhere you feel is right will work. Play right in the center, on the edges, or at a distance where you can watch your cycles. Weigh in any place that strikes a chord that resonates with you. If you have favorite music, I suggest that you listen to it as you place your magical scale in YOUR WHEEL. It will brighten your perspective here!

Keep your eyes open today. Is there something valuable to notice? When you simply notice something here it is like a small discovery. Feel the joy of change that small discoveries bring with them. Place yourself where you want to be today and flow naturally without force. As you work and play today, or tomorrow if you are going to dream some first, think only of the things you are doing. Reasons may go wonderfully missing here today. Reasons can always return. Right now simply enjoy things and be amazed how many cool things come together. Enjoy things at the best time for you. Be aware and enjoy things that simply happen as they do.

YOUR WHEEL and your magical scales and all the gifts you have been given already have natural places here. No need to rush and move them. As YOUR WHEEL keeps cycling like the tires on your bicycle, feel the perspective you have unfold discovery along the path to the places you go. You will find places that feel just right for your Imagination Tools as you go along.

Welcome to THE WHEEL! Welcome to YOUR WHEEL! Hop on. Find a Ferris Wheel or a merry-go-round! They are together here. Settle in and enjoy the ride. Notice the scenery as we slowly go round and round. Notice what you saw before in a new way each time you see it again. Things may change a little or a lot. Simply notice them and be considerate of their life force. The things you experience are yours to feel. Develop them as you see fit.

I am THE WHEEL OF FORTUNE. I am not a thing really. I am the love of big things that come together. I am the love of the big things of luck and change. I am also the love of fortune and abundance. I am the orbit of each and every planet and star. I feel these orbits are all the big things that happiness and prosperity like. Enjoy a love of return while you are here! My BIGGEST love is when you complete something and it refreshes your perspective! Return here to refresh when you feel different in a familiar place.

⇒ *Imagination Tool* From The Wheel
(Now *Your* Wheel)

- I give you a place to put your magical scale and other tools. I give you the gift that I am also an Imagination Toolbox. I will always change to magically fit the new tools you create, discover, and are given as you go along. And, you can utilize me to tune your perspective as you complete things. Your Imagination Toolbox as Your Wheel is for everything that keeps your perspective clear and fresh. Enjoy the Imagination Toolbox of Your Wheel.

XI Strength

Strength indicates that you master self-control as you tame your fears and harness your impulses. The power of your voice is important in Strength. Feel infinite fortitude while you incorporate your voice. Visualize how a sprinter sits, how a lion lounges or naps. Strength itself is not indicated to tame your beast. Strength here is to harness your voice. A simple way is indicated. Simple gestures establish direction. Your strength is natural. Anything more than necessary may cause decay or damage. Just enough is all you need here.

Understand that you are very powerful at this time. Be mindful of others. You play with more power than you may know. Speak and act only as you need at this time. Understand that your presence is felt without bluster or backlash.

Mastery of self-control that harnesses your fears and impulses can be the core of what drives you. Think, "I boldly go." And, go forth here with heart and infinite fortitude. Speak with self-restraint as you complete things and put more things together. Strength is always serious, and also always joking. Think of a sprinter that sits, a lion that naps. That is Strength. If no action is made, that may still express your decisions. You can feel power and beauty in the sprinter and the lion even as they sit or nap.

Remember that Strength is a card of mind and body that are joined to work together. Strength does not mean

Strength
Self-control, voice, simplicity

to tame the beast, but to tune the voice. STRENGTH is the presence to walk up and plop as a beast clearly and naturally. STRENGTH is your natural voice. Like likes like. Think on this.

STRENGTH indicates you are full of life as a hunter of old and a housekeeper of old. A hunter of old leaves home for the hunt with no more than anything inside or outside that was necessary. The house of old was kept with no more than anything necessary inside or outside. STRENGTH indicates that a simple way is best. Simple steps establish direction with natural strength. You feel nothing overly sensational to bait you forth too quickly, nothing bad to yoke you back. The movements of your voice are simple and clear without fetter. Feel the natural steps of your voice as you speak in only the way you can. Your voice is yours. Know that your presence is felt without threat, recourse, or question. Something positive can be done for someone anonymously. Do it. Smile. Then, put it out of your mind. That has voice as well.

Enter Strength

Sit with us here. Relax and sit as a sprinter sits. Speak your perspective. Sit as a lion lounges. Relish in all the new perspectives you have to look forward to from YOUR WHEEL. We are in no hurry here. Our STRENGTH is a subtle energy like sunlight. It is constant, and when gone it is always soon to return. We voice things like the sun always shines. Sometimes we speak brightly. Sometimes we whisper from behind clouds. Even at night THE MOON steps in to reflect our voice in another way. We work together to expand the breadth of your voice. When we rest, our brightness goes into our dreams, thoughts, and ideas. The Hermit taught us that. We know our brightness is soon to return each morning as we wake.

Practice your studies and work to voice your ideas. Feel the Strength of ideas. Feel the power of voice. Things happen here and there and further along your way that were never even dreamed when your voice is strong. Be vigorous and disciplined and learn something new as pleasant surprises arrive. Here in Mystereum you will be introduced to The World. It is our biggest Wheel. For now simply sit with us and practice your voice from your perspective.

We would like you to clearly express the perspective of the ideas that are on your mind. We would like you to practice your creative voice.

⇒ *Imagination Tools* From Strength

- We give you a strong and calm place to practice your creative voice. This is not the action. This is a place to prepare to be able to hop up and get into the action where you stand and deliver!

- We give you an exercise to strengthen your clarity for your creative voice. Check with a doctor to make sure it is okay for you to participate in this exercise before you do it. We only want the best for you.

1. Inhale for 4 counts and think of energy and the element fire.
2. Hold for 4 counts and think of fulfillment and the element water.
3. Exhale for 4 counts and think of communication and the element air.
4. Hold for 4 counts with your lungs empty and think of a clean home and the element earth.
5. Count to 5 whispering your count out loud across one long exhale.
6. Count to 5 whispering your count out loud across one long inhale. You might laugh, too, as you do this one.
7. Repeat this breathing sequence 5 times. Then express an idea to practice your perspective. Say, write down, and/or sketch your idea. Voice it and enjoy!

XII The Hanged Man

THE HANGED MAN indicates that you may be afloat in clarity. Your spirituality, dreams, and intuition are heightened and clearly sensed. Suspension is also indicated. This suspension is often very peaceful and not suffering. It is often a feeling of total support like when you float in water.

THE HANGED MAN indicates to stop resistance. Make yourself vulnerable to the influence of positive things. In doing so you may glimpse illumination. Very deep insight is indicated. Even if but for a moment, nothing but that insight will feel to exist. And, as timeless as that moment seems, you may have an acute awareness of its temporary nature. Note your insights at this time however great or small they are. Remember them and this time. The memory of their presence can remain strong. You may feel forever changed by a HANGED MAN experience.

THE HANGED MAN indicates spirituality, dreams, intuition, psychic abilities, and that you are afloat in them. With THE WHEEL you are given awareness and begin to fasten experiences to your Imagination Tool belt. With THE WORLD you will be gifted infinite places for your ideas. With THE HANGED MAN you are conscious of the divinity of your inner infinity as a real thing. One thing is certain with THE HANGED MAN. Whether your insights are great or small, spiritual or mundane, once you have experienced THE HANGED MAN, you never see things

The Hanged Man
Afloat, clarity, vision

quite the same. 12 mirrors 21 visually. With THE WORLD (21, XXI) you can go infinitely out and feel everything around you. With THE HANGED MAN (12, XII) you can go infinitely in as you feel chords struck that resonate throughout your whole being. Peaceful, this is a place of suspension. This is not life or death. Here resistance has stopped. Illumination is available.

Enter The Hanged Man

Hey there! Up here in the tree! Welcome! Do you like playing on the jungle gym? Do you like climbing and hangin' out? I sure do! I hear you have a message for me from my Mom, THE EMPRESS. Cool, Kewel! What is it?!

Climb on up in your mind and hang out with me. Your imagination is the best and safest first place for things like this. You do not need to be concerned about these ropes. They are loose! I imagined them there so I could really see and feel the connection between my hands and between my foot and my favorite tree! It grew from my heart! You may have noticed that my Mom, THE EMPRESS, is a tree. So is my Dad's magical horse. He's funny to me. Sometimes he is on his horse. Then, when it turns into a tree, he sometimes rides inside and looks out through the knot hole. I like that, and I still find it kind of hilarious.

My Dad, THE EMPEROR, taught me to sit down to feel more grounded. He taught me to focus on my roots. I gave that to STRENGTH, though. I like relaxin' and hangin' out much better. So, I came up with this idea of my *Hangin' Around Tree*. I was sitting with his horse when the idea came to me, and I followed my heart. Sometimes I hang out from simple wood, too. As long as it grew from the earth and lives with mutual respect of others and does not have splinters, I like hangin' around with it.

I am THE HANGED MAN. I love my spirituality and my dreams and my psychic abilities. You might call them intuition. That's cool. Psychic, though, for me feels to get more to where they are at. There is no door or portal for me to go through to sense them. I swim in them naturally at will. They are full-on rockin'!

My first love is being wholly present as I swim and float-fly through my infinite imagination. I love it even if it is simply for a short moment. It is very refreshing. I always discover something new, or something I do feels refreshed. I love the experience of being afloat inside while I am hangin' around here. My imagination is and will always be very real to me. I live with a foot in each world. It is my way. I like that a lot.

Oh! Thanks for the message from my Mom! Think I will hang out up here for a while longer as I smile to her in my mind. Her leaves will rustle nicely as she smiles back. Her leaves are like aspen tree leaves. They sound like running water when they rustle. Thank you. I appreciate that you remembered.

My insights are temporary like the top of a mountain on a hike. They are magical, though. They feel majestic like a place I surely cannot be, but most certainly am. Remember that a HANGED MAN moment may be a temporary experience on your path. But, it sure will not be forgettable! The place and experience these moments make always remain in my memory. They remain like when you meet a new friend.

I am friends with enlightenment. We hang out once in a while very regularly. You can, too. Enlightenment told me that your brightness could make a lighthouse. Please remember that. It can guide you away from trouble. And, I ask you to remember this place and time without dwelling on it too much. Think of inner lemonade on a psychic, summer day. This time will pass, but not just yet. Let it strike chords that resonate fully! Hear them through and through.

One thing is certain. Whether my insights have been great or small, spiritual or mundane. . .some people say earthly. . .once I have them, I never see things quite the same. Cool, Kewel, huh?! Hang out with me for a while. Your journey is your gig, ya know?!

⇒ *IMAGINATION TOOLS*
FROM THE HANGED MAN

- I give a place of your own to clearly float in your mind.
- I introduce you to illumination. Hang out with it once in a while.
- I gift you a place to hang your idea solar system in these rings. I suggest you create orbits for your biggest ideas so they move naturally.
- THE WHEEL mentioned to suggest that you play with your magical scale here when you want, too. It moves smoother here without resistance.
- I gift you perspective for your play here so your play gives you more to explore later. For now, simply experience the insights you have while hangin' out here.

OH! STRENGTH's lion tried to hang by his tail once here and chat with me. *Uh hem.* Let's just say he felt more comfortable on the ground and hanging his paws over the branches when he climbed up again. ☺ That gave us both a great laugh. He is a funny cat.

He already had a different inner light than I have. STRENGTH brings him to hang out here once in a while. I dig their way a lot! They are really natural. When they hang out here, their voices resonate really well!

XIII Death

DEATH indicates transformation and sweeping change. It is indicated to sacrifice unnecessary preconceptions that you hold and evolve. Your Phoenix rises. DEATH can be birth's introduction. It is a preamble like in the Constitution. Visualize a garden in the wintertime where things rest. Natural patience and renewal are virtues of the DEATH card. Your perennial ideas and actions naturalize like flowers in a garden here. This way they come back in more vibrantly each year! Haste is not indicated. Slow your pace and be fully present as things unfold.

If you are distressed at this time, please mind your time and your placements. Do not trample on the subtle, new things in your life no matter how small they appear. Notice them. Focus on the new and fragile details and nurture them. Renewal awakens slowly. More is present than meets the eye.

DEATH indicates that you yourself are the Phoenix. Life and death are the same thing here, or one thing. They are together as a birth-and-death. DEATH itself can be birth's introduction, its preamble. There is another field trip for you. Play with "preamble." Look at the preamble to The Constitution. DEATH also indicates to sacrifice the preconceptions of your old world, the old you. This can refresh you.

DEATH is a card of the winter garden where things rest to renew. This rest, or removal of what you have come

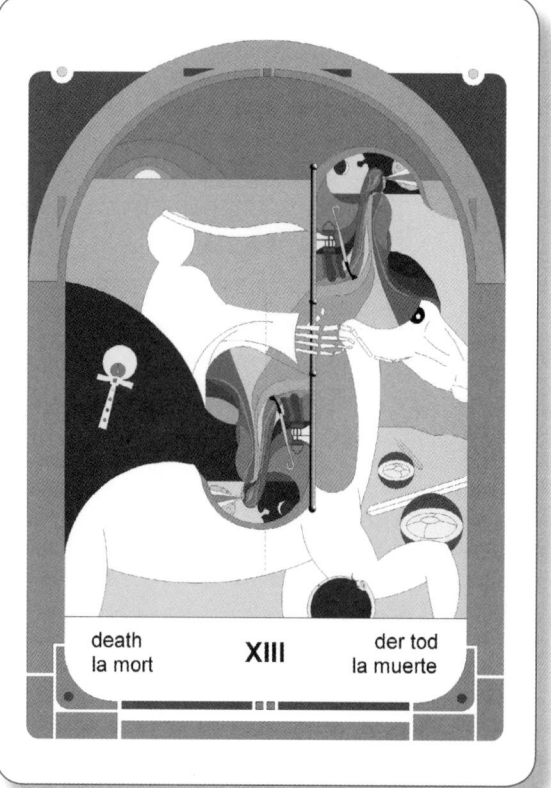

Death
Transformation, Phoenix, renewal

to expect, makes for a future surge in your growth. In a garden, perennials naturalize to come back in more places. You also naturalize. You will feel different placements over your seasons.

The DEATH card indicates a place of transformations. Think of a chrysalis made by a butterfly. Note the not so subtle things that go on inside it. THE EMPEROR goes step by step so that even in surprise he is able to re-align the whole system in a single step. THE EMPEROR's process can inform the DEATH card at a very small and natural scale like a butterfly. Do not apply force to re-align your whole system at this time, though. Know and feel the re-alignment that takes place. Be aware and sensitive. Be patient. Be present with your idea solar system. This will prepare you for your transformations to bloom.

DEATH indicates that transformation and change present themselves all on their own. Force is not indicated here. Be comfortable with the *not-knowing* and flow with your renewal. Your newness will awaken just as you do each morning.

If you feel disruption, it may present as frustration. That is okay. Look to the small things that are still. Look to the small things that rest and sleep. Look to THE HANGED MAN to increase your vision. Look forward to Temperance to feel all things together as one world while you respect the small things. Imagine this and it will be so!

Enter Death

First off, Hi. You need not hold your breath here. Trust your gut. I feel that you do not need to be afraid. As DEATH I am all about transformation. Yes, things certainly live and die in cycles. Here in your wonderful imagination, though, I am here to keep your ideas fresh. I love to think about gardens and flowers that come back to bloom each year. They are called perennials. Your ideas are perennial, too. You see, in a garden, I do a lot of work at a very small scale. A leaf falls here, a twig from a tree falls there. All the while this helps the flowers and trees and plants to spend their precious energy to shine in all their glory.

I work with movement. I will give you your Imagination Tool as a sprout before I tell you a little more about myself. Then, I will give you the same gift afterwards, but transformed as a fresh fruit-blossom to enjoy.

I give you the Imagination Tool sprout of a whole different kind of perspective. Here goes! "Depletion indicates misspent efforts." Is that really big or really small? Once you find places of depletion, call on me to remove the parts of it that hold you back. You will know these because they are not peaceful in their sleep. You will know them because they do not give in return. It will not always be me who comes to help you clean and freshen your imagination when you call. Oftentimes, I will send other characters that will be the best for the job.

Think of gasoline and a car. Under the right circumstances they do their job. But, the gas is burned and the waste goes out the exhaust. That is waste. Then, you fill up the tank again. I do not like waste. I like cars, but I use fallen leaves and twigs to nourish my ground. They make more energy to keep the shine and colors bright. I feel it is better that people nourish ideas and tend to both with powerful witness. The healthy leaves and branches in your daily life are like your ideas. I like them to shine and be vivid and grow.

I advise that if you are angry, do not prune things. I did it once in a garden, and I cut a rose bush back too hard. I will never forget that. It took it years to recover. It was not ready to fall. Now, I am sensitive to tune and tailor things as I go along. You see I like fresh things. Call me a filter. Change me once in a while. I like your imagination to stay fresh. I am transformation. I am your invisible support system. Remember your orbits in your idea solar system. I am the marriage of things that bridge with each other. I suggest that you nurture and tune and tailor your ideas to keep your life fresh. This is what I do.

☙ *IMAGINATION TOOLS* FROM DEATH

- I give to you the Imagination Tool of "Depletion indicates misspent efforts." This is where you forget the things that deplete you and drain you. Outright drop them like leaves from a tree. That is an Imagination Tool sprout I give you.

- Run around and play and breathe deeply. This is fun that fills you up! This is your Imagination Tool sprout in full bloom! Play can make a bridge. Laughter often shortens the bridge and brings things together.

XIV Temperance

TEMPERANCE indicates that things above and below mix and work together. Think of the centaur Chiron. Think of a person and animal joined as a uniquely complete being. See Chiron's bow and arrow. Think of a person and their ideas joined as a uniquely complete being. The bow draws back the stationary arrow. Let go of the string and the arrow flies from the stationary bow. Feel the bow and arrow's movements mix things to work together to connect and nourish your sense of direction. A strong sequence is indicated. When ideas are in play, the personalities you give them points to their support structures. Your idea solar system's orbits work with a natural balance here. Your actions expand and pulse with life. Your actions are like your own, personal elements. Put them together.

To strike a balance is also indicated. Take everything you have in moderation, including moderation sometimes. Moderation can simply be a blend of well-balanced and harmonious ideas. Enjoy this strong time where your biggest ideas and dreams, your daily grind, and your rush-rush activities may feel just right together! Your ideas work together in wonderful balance. They have their natural places like planets' orbits. This is the card where unity becomes identity, and identity transforms to reinforce the balance of your ideas.

Temperance
Mixing, balance, duet

The movements of TEMPERANCE repeat through your life! THE FOOL is the Narrator, the one who starts the journey through things. The TEMPERANCE card IS everything! They are partners! Feel your ideas connect and light up throughout your idea solar system! Your inside and outside worlds connect and balance. Dream bigger with TEMPERANCE! There are no limits to what you can do now!

The TEMPERANCE card is often brought to a very human level. Here, outside of its archetypal home, it can indicate moderation. And, that is important. THE HIEROPHANT brought spirit to the earth. Temperance brings spirit to join with your body in each deep breath. This is about moderation and also about balance. Think incorporation. Think integration. Think harmony. Think of a blend with voices intact. Think duet. Remember the reserves of energy that a sprinter who sits has. Remember the lion's nap. STRENGTH is full-on still present.

TEMPERANCE indicates that you feel things in motion rather than feel their differences. Think of a rainbow. Think rain. Think bow. Think arrow. Remember the divine tools of the Archer. Let the colorful rainbow smile a light on your aim.

Enter Temperance

I am her above. I am also him below. We work together. Hi from both of us together! Remember THE LOVERS earlier! They gifted you a vibrant partnership with your bow of STRENGTH and your arrow of direction. They also gave you a bow of respect. We are like them in a way. We simply work on a much larger scale! And, you have your magical scale! Imagine it even bigger across the whole of your imagination to weigh us into your Mystereum mix.

Okay (as they chuckle a little). Pardon, we need to introduce ourselves a little more before we continue our excitement and move forward. We are really glad you are here to freshen our mix! We use all of the tools in Mystereum. We also usually use them all the time. OH BOY, do we know that is a lot to ask. But, we realized long ago that the identity of our talent was just that. We love that in each of our ways we work together! Some things live above. Some things live below. Some always move freshly and are alive back and forth between both. We will let you find those things for yourself. We keep things in a living and mutual balance.

DEATH expressed to you the movement of a leaf that falls to the ground. As the leaf breaks down in the ground it nourishes flowers and trees. This describes some of our movements. More than a single leaf, though, we do that for you with everything in Mystereum, above and below. Spend some time and let your eyes move around our picture. Trace our path in our card. Do you see a calligraphy character outlined by the way we flow? We wish to show you how dynamic the balance is in your imagination.

We love to see opposites merge in ways where they balance each other in harmony. Remember THE CHARIOT, but bigger! We work with him a great deal. Think of Chiron. Please take a field trip to check out Chiron's story! He is all about Sagittarius. So are we! All twelve astrological signs have a place here. We will let that be a story for another day.

Enjoy your field trip to check out Chiron! Let your imagination and your actions be like a bow and arrows that bow. We feel they will work together with respect. Feel their energies as they guide you like stars in the sky. Hmmm, star constellations in your imagination? Sound familiar? Are you having fun here?! ☺

⇒ IMAGINATION TOOLS FROM TEMPERANCE

- You have the freedom to look around and see bigger things!
- Sense and feel what makes you a wonderful, uniquely complete being.
- You are not alone. Express your ideas. Meet your support.

We smile and feel how vibrant and unique you are! Remember our mutual respect for each other. We have that for you, too. Stuff is about to start really movin' and shakin' in Mystereum soon! We want you to be ready for it all. Take some deep breaths and get your smile rockin'!

It is almost night here in Mystereum. We are a card of the bridge that is dawn and also dusk. Remember us in the small places between things. Does darkness rise or fall? Is dusk DEATH for the day? Is dawn DEATH for the night? Ride THE MOON through the night in your dreams to the dawn. Let THE SUN brighten your day. We are in them both. We are everywhere. We live in both the dusk and the dawn. We are together in twilight, moonlight, and sunlight regardless of clouds. There is this one goofy word we dig a lot! Interstice. We find that word very interesting, like twilight.

XV The Devil

THE DEVIL card in one way indicates the power of your expectations with focus rather than blind spots. THE DEVIL is not "Satan." THE DEVIL here is Pan. He is a half-goat, nature-god. Some call him Dionysus. Others call him Bacchus. Pleasure, and to happily let go in wild, unbridled play is indicated. This is not unrequited play. It is unbridled and free of worry. Temptation may be indicated. Ambition is indicated more. Temptation often leaves as expansive possibilities that please you arrive.

THE DEVIL can indicate a rise of earthly desires in you. Mind that these feelings are not to be ashamed of or to fear. If you are compassionate with yourself and others, odds are that your desires are great things. Inhibitions can hold you back and enslave you as easily as excess when do too much. Your expectations can make blind spots. They can also provide a magical focus on the invisible connections between things. Be mindful of your intensity here. Things that held you back are loose. Do not be taken by surprise by your intensity. Use the greater freedom for mobility and explore larger feelings. Have a feast with friends!

A feast is not necessarily gluttony. It can be wonderful and vibrant fun where you spread your energetic wealth. Enjoy a devilish, exquisite meal that you love. Enjoy an excited bike ride in the park! There is great fuel to be had in FUN! Enjoy yourself! Remember TEMPERANCE as you are mindful

The Devil
Ambition, pleasure, intensity

of your intensity so you do not slide around out of control. Again, do not let your intensity take you by surprise. Sense what is intense and be highly aware of its energy. Intensity is much like when your identity is fully present.

Odds are you are not mean. If you are not mean, it is dang hard to make decisions or act anything NEAR mean. That sure is amazing! So, smile, let go, and be amazed with yourself and your ideas!

THE DEVIL's experience is not always pleasurable. Neither are strings of mediocrity. It is indicated to enjoy your feelings in your actions. Abolish the toxins of your fears. Feel the purity of your desires. Experience emancipation! Free your ideas!

Ambition can be frightening and dangerous. And, it can be less frightening and dangerous than idle hands. Someone with a Midas Touch may starve their soul. But, that is doubtful. That person can also afford a five-course dinner for friends that puts the life right back in everyone! It is indicated to be honest and enjoy yourself as you open up! Chains or brakes you feel may serve to keep you in one place long enough to warm up.

Here is a point of interest to THE DEVIL in Mystereum. THE DEVIL's understanding is that the Tibetans do not have a word in their language for the concept of guilt. They have responsibility and intensity in spades. A miser's gold is much like idle hands. A miser has splendor that suffocates glory. Idle hands suffocate the glory of splendor. Instead of all that, energize your actions with your intensity. Remember the sprinter. Now, feel the sprint! Remember the lion. Feel the strength! With smooth and strong stretches and no harm, unleash!

Enter The Devil

Huuuuurrrrrooooo!!!!! How RRRRR UUUUU? I am not THAT devil. I am not Satan. I am a deity more like Pan. Pan is a half-goat, nature-god. I will hang back a little and let that settle in for you. Proceed when you feel ready.

You can take a field trip for Pan like you did to see Chiron if you would like. They are both quite interesting characters. People also attuned with an animal. Hmmm.

Let me tell you about myself from my intense perspective. By myself I am like a goat. If you have ever been in a goat pen, you already know this. Look me in the eye and 4 seconds, 5 seconds later BAM! I will zip over and butt you with my horns. Goats are about full-on ego and pecking order. Fortunately, though, that is not all of me. Those two people here who do not tell me their names are visiting from TEMPERANCE. They add another dimension to my identity. You see, between her on the left and him on the right, they have tempered my goat-ego. You will see tempering further with your SWORDS. My goat-ego is primal. It tries to establish hierarchies. Hierarchies are pecking orders. With those two here, my ego realizes that pecking and head-butting does not create much good order, or at least order that lasts very long. Those two visit from TEMPERANCE and are really like my hands. They came to show me my earthly desires in action. I am grateful that I was able to arrive in Mystereum after TEMPERANCE. That way I could be amazed to receive the gift of my desires in action! My ego simply arranges and places things. The couple from TEMPERANCE are here to guide me and activate my placements.

You see a long time ago I went too far all the time. It started to scare me. Then, I started not to go far enough ever. Sometimes I would act out with my excesses. Sometimes I would hide and stuff things inside my inhibitions. I thought everything was hidden. But, that did not feel right for me. There were things I wanted to do that I had been told were wrong. Someone told me not to use my purple crayon on my black and white drawing. I was told "no," and something about that kind of "no" bothered me. It was my art, right?! I was excited to use my purple crayon! But, I took it to heart and my excitement deflated. It was not like when my parents told me not to cross the street by myself. That was important! Glad they did! Or, later with them not to cross the street without looking both ways and keep my eyes and ears open. Those things are important! When TEMPERANCE came here that first night, I began to learn from the greatest teachers of all. I began to learn from life and myself. Now, my life is my best teacher, and I learn from others even more than before. It took a lot of work. But, now I am the best teacher to feel what is right for me. That strengthens my ears, too. There is not so much chatter of worry. I listen better now because I am sure of myself. And, I do not haggle and reduce my desires.

TEMPERANCE brought choices to my goat-ego. They helped me learn about myself and put the uniquely complete being that is ME into action! Now, what I want is not about what simply feels good. Now what I want feels good across the board and continues into the future. Vroooom! Vroooooooommmmmmm!

➣ IMAGINATION TOOLS
FROM THE DEVIL

- I give to you the Imagination Tool of the freedom to feel your desires clearly. Explore them and strike your own balances and do no harm.

- I also give you an unlimited four-season-per-year-night-n-day pass to hang with THE HANGED MAN. You are already welcome there, of course. But, I want to give you what TEMPERANCE gave me. They suggested I hang there for a bit if I feel perplexed. That has shown me when perplexed is a natural feeling that indicates "to stop," or to say "no," or that I simply need a different perspective and all is just fine. It has also shown me when things are simply new, and when to step on the gas!

I suggest hangin' with THE HANGED MAN. Re-visit TEMPERANCE between here and there before you move on. After you visit them, come back through here and hold on to your hat! A big roller coaster is on its way!

XVI The Tower

It is the middle of the night in Mystereum. THE FOOL feels a big dream and hops on Fabric to fly back to the castle. The castle had been kept fresh. But, THE FOOL left it untended. The castle had grown into THE TOWER. THE TOWER grew higher and higher. It began to only have hoarded gold and riches and idle hands. Wild and uninvited partygoers filled the top. This angered THE FOOL.

"This is unfitting for my castle!" THE FOOL said. THE FOOL's voice became a big, lightning bolt of truth and blasted the whole structure to rubble! Everything changed! The castle was gone.

As the smoke cleared, a small child in a green meadow appeared where the castle once was. It then felt like daytime in the dream. Moving nearer, the child began asking THE FOOL questions about life and death and everything in the universe.

THE FOOL is patient and attentive and warms to the child answering each and every question. THE FOOL think-feels in the dream, "I feel I KNOW ALL the answers to this child's questions of everything!"

The child becomes silent at this dream-thought. The sudden silence startles THE FOOL.

The Tower
Big change, world-altering, emancipating

Politely, THE FOOL asks, "Who are you?" The child's eyes glimmer brightly with a smile saying, "I am you, only new!"

THE FOOL feels fresh and new with a bright smile. THE FOOL becomes the maker of the huge transformation!

THE TOWER indicates big change! Change is indicated that changes your whole life! Your pond turns over so to speak. Your resistance to change has been torn down suddenly. False structures and beliefs crash down! Their crash is sudden, violent, and all at once. Grief may be present. This is natural. Be mindful not to re-hydrate your old fears. They fall of their own accord with the old structures. Once the air has cleared breathe in the change. Take in what remains. You may have just dismissed the shackles of being single-minded!

No-one said this place is easy. Your whole life may turn upside down. But, smile and sense the opportunity to discover new treasures. You are you, only new! You are the new treasure! You may have just let go of the dreams and whole structures of things that did not work for you! You may have just accomplished your dreams. Shine the brightness of your smile as you begin to see anew.

A pond turning over is a stinky and tumultuous event. Though the pond may be more fertile the next day, the next day is not yet here. For your own sake, and take this to heart, remember that throughout the duration of the event, the pond is still a pond. You are still you! Search yourself.

Treasured truths unfold for you to discover. Look to THE DEVIL for courage. Breathe in your change with courage. Trust yourself. Smile. Dream. Build. This could take a while. What do your strokes look like now? Smile as you move in a new way. You are you, only new!

Take care with your ideas. They are indicated to be new and unfamiliar. THE FOOL's lightning bolt has already struck. Do not be surprised if other people or your own ideas dispel your illusions in a flash. Odds are, you are knocked off any pedestals like a bolt out of the blue. Get your feet on the solid ground. Take a walk. Breathe deep and step up to the plate. Time is always limited. And, timing here has more to do with thoughtful communication in fresh action.

Enter The Tower

Wear your hard hat here! Also, wear your work gloves and safety goggles! They are already there in your mind. Please put them on first. As long as you have your safety gear on, you are welcome here. Make them the color or colors you want. Hazard Yellow is good. Make them comfortable and visible. A lot is going on here. Ponds are turning over. Structures past their service-life crumble and crash down fast!

I am THE TOWER. I am another place of creation. I take place right before you make rockin' new gestures with your ideas on a blank, new page! You see my part of Mystereum is to make huge transformation possible. We do the work here quickly and all at once. See THE CHARIOT pull! We work like when you rip off a band-aid that is not stuck to your boo boo. Quick! But, do not hurt yourself more when you do.

We clean up our mess up just as quickly, too. It almost disintegrates like it was never there. That way the new, tiny, little sprouts of ideas and moonbeam glimmers of dreams can see the light and be seen as they burst back up into the light! Remember the Phoenix that DEATH mentioned. That Phoenix lives here. It is never seen, though. The Phoenix is the personality of our place. It is the spirit of our place, our form of genius. Your spirit grows here from the core as ideas that are dead weight fall away. Tailor your new edges in a big way. This place is not easy. But, you may broaden your perspective with the experience. Remember the power of this time. It will serve you and those you care for well.

Most important here is your imagination. Keep it under your hard hat and in your mind's eye. You may sense many glimmers of hope that come together after the smoke clears. They are like little candles. They are like stars in your sky. Feel this and sense THE STAR that comes up soon in Mystereum. For now I simply ask you to bring a single star into focus in your mind. Find a star of your own. Find something to go with it that calms you. It is VERY noisy in here a lot. Stay aware. Find the quiet. Focus on your star and be patient.

When you are ready, simply nod. You can continue then. Do not go in to this tower. It is ready to blow already as your truth makes it happen. Take a deep breath. You are about to be the boss here! Your changes are yours! Do not hesitate to ask another for perspective or ideas. Do not be afraid to ask yourself, either. We need you fully present to proceed and maintain your safety, and for you to get the full benefit. You will clear your playing field here so you can see a new start more fully on your own. Let us know when you are good and ready. Thanks!

The Tower comes down when depletions are left unchecked and many things are out of balance. Many sprouts burst forth under The Tower. It is only a natural matter of time before these things shake The Tower apart to be removed. Worry will not be heard here. It is too loud in here. Let go and feel the truth of your many sprouts burst forth in your voice! Let the smoke clear. Then, move anew.

⇒ *Imagination Tools* From The Tower

- I give you the Imagination Tool to be fully present and protected as you weather big storms of change that rain inside and out.
- I give you a powerful silence to be calm and patient until the smoke and rubble clear. In your powerful silence sense The Star rise from the hot blast of The Phoenix! It is yours! It is large and close-up! It welcomes you! Fly to The Star as The Fool flew in for you here! You can leave the lightning here. Keep the truth.

XVII The Star

The Star indicates that you find your cosmic groove and go for it! Eternal hope in the diamond-like seat of your *mindbodybeautiful* is indicated to sparkle brightly! Your presence and memories are vibrant. Your hope and your knowledge are strong!

The Star encourages you to shift focus and re-position your magical scale. There is no need to move your gaze from your focus as you do this. Imagine the movement. The Star indicates vibrant momentum that you re-orchestrate! Even the smallest star provides a glimmer of hope. This is a bright time to feel your ideas expand. The Star is the card of eternal hope. It is the diamond-like seat of your mind and your body. It represents the living spirit of your *mindbodybeautiful*! The strength of your eternal hope guides you to find your cosmic groove and go for it!

That one star you focused on with The Tower now becomes the ultimate star right in front of you. It has become The Star! Keep it in sight and in fresh focus. Re-direct your magical scale to feel it more fully. Study it. It may become a star that also has whole new worlds orbiting around it. They are there to expand your belief in the brightness of your ideas. Feel the subtle star that was your focus as it grows closer and inspires you! Bask in its glow as you increase yours! A candle might eclipse this light at first before it grows. A candle may also enhance this light and bring it closer. Let it light itself and sit in your mind as you breathe deep and slow. Like your castle, do not leave your candle unattended.

The Magician simply took a spark to show you. The Star's hope builds this spark more brightly across your journey. Find your cosmic groove with The Star's eternal sense of hope and go for it from there!

The Star indicates the permanent presence of your possibilities, your memories, your hope, and your knowledge. No matter its size, tiny or ginormous, may it light your mind. It is always there. It lives in your cosmic groove. It gives you a light of hope no matter how far away it is, no matter how dark it feels around you. This is the card of eternal hope. It is the diamond-like seat of the mind and body. It is the spirit of your *mindbodybeautiful*! Feel the magic genies in faraway stars. Let them receive your wishes.

Do not breathe in false hope. Give fictions to The Moon. It will arrive soon and will reflect them elsewhere. Be patient and mindful of the stillness in your pinpoint of hopeful light. Remember your glass of water on your lake. Let all these little lights slowly sparkle together as they burst forward from your perspective.

Enter The Star

I smile to you from your Mystereum night sky. In my smile is eternal hope where all good are things welcome. I begin to show you to how to find and *express* your cosmic groove, your highest purpose. I am simple. I am far away.

The Star
Cosmic grooves, eternal hope, inspiration

I am near in your imagination. My light travels thousands of years to reach you each night as you stream forth your wishes for me to receive.

I am simple. From all the way across the universe I wish eternal hope to you. I hope that you keep your cosmic groove fresh! What card comes before me? What card comes after me? Let them fall away and sleep while you settle in your most important pinpoint of inner light. Feel what you feel right now! Feel the verbs of the cards as they move in and through you to inform your situations. Feel how they move, just like you see how I shine. Are some of your Imagination Tools similar to one another? Is there any way they are all the same? Visit here when you want to turn up your inspiration. I can help you find light that travels forever to reach you now!

I am so big and so there that "way far away" may feel like you can reach out and touch your eternal hope every night in the sky right here. Feel your bright hope shine in the inner night of your imagination. I am always here for you. I am eternal. I am eternal hope.

I love for you to find your cosmic groove and go for it!

I love your eternal hope that is bright and shines as the spirit of your *mindbodybeautiful*!

I am here in the inner stars of your ideas.

I am so bright because your ideas inspire me!

Smile up to me here in your sky. Like your imagination, I am always here.

⇒ IMAGINATION TOOLS FROM THE STAR

- Mystereum is a wonderfully big place with many discoveries to make, and new ones come all the time. I send you eternal glimmers of hope to light your way through any darkness. Use them how you please for your highest good.
- I wish you a vivid imagination even in the darkest night to awaken your dreams and continue to find your cosmic groove!
- A gift of directions. THE TOWER was blasted down to the ground. I send great light and eternal hope across the universe to light up your ideas.

XVIII The Moon

Some of the things that THE MOON indicates are vision, illusion, madness, genius, and poetry. THE MOON is like bright eyes that peer from the darkness in the night sky. THE MOON card also indicates inner connections so intense that they magnetically transcend space. This is the kind of intense intuition that joins a variety of unseen forces. It reflects them inside and out. Creative connections with things that seem impossible can also be indicated. The intensity and power of reflection indicated by THE MOON can be felt in many ways. THE MOON's reflection on a watery path can disorient you or fascinate and mesmerize you with a beautiful image.

"Disorient" and "mesmerize" are related concepts. Feel into your personal experiences with THE MOON. Feel from your own shadow where your eyes glow like the moon at night. THE MOON indicates to trust your intuition without fail. It indicates that to simply believe and to know are not enough. THE MOON feels its own personality as it reflects THE SUN. Planning is for another time. Your planning may already have placed you right where you are now! Enjoy this as a surprise. Move with only the natural motions of your ideas in mind. Sense your magnetism as you reflect them.

THE MOON can also indicate misplacement to the degree that you wonder why there are all these vegetables around you when you purchased front row seats. Be where you are or skidaddle to where you need to be. Or, enjoy the show

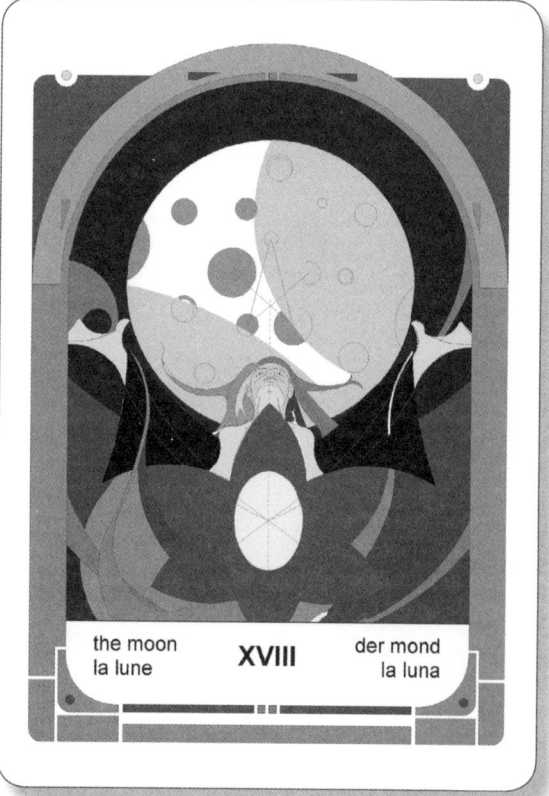

The Moon
Vision, genius, poetry

with some fruit from a different perspective. To believe and to know are not enough with THE MOON. It is indicated to trust your intuition without fail.

Enter The Moon

Welcome to my place of the night in Mystereum. You just met THE STAR. You met DEATH at twilight as the sun began to move across the horizon between the night and the day. I shine to light up your Mystereum sky along with THE STAR. Cool thing? There are no time zones in Mystereum! We are always here for you in just the ways that you need us to be so we can help you reflect the poetry of your ideas with the genius of your imagination.

Raise your hands and lift your ideas to me. Bask in the way I reflect them. Notice how I work with you and transform your light. Notice how the sun is a warm color during the day with gold and red and orange. I reflect this in a unique way at night. I often transform warm sunlight colors to cool colors at night when I am up in the sky farther from the horizon. These cool colors may feel like white that is tinted with green or blue. I show you the depths of night as I reflect.

I especially love it when this happens around Halloween. I often become a harvest moon and shine big with bright gold amber. At that time you may feel me even more clearly as I bring the clarity of the day right into the depths of your night. Simply gaze upon me. That can be our conversation. Speak if you wish. I will watch over you in the night. When I am not visible, close your eyes and see further inside. Look into your imagination and you will find me. Sometimes I rest from the night to be in other peoples' day sky.

I have a favorite madness. My favorite madness is people who can laugh without reason. I think they have either found a path to enlightenment or have gone completely crazy. Their laughter tells me which. I sense everyone here in Mystereum from up here in the day and night sky. I watch and enjoy as they play and frolic. I see how bright their eyes are in the night. I see how much brighter they are when they laugh. I love to be the reflective one. I love to be the magnetic one. And, there is my gift to you. I show you a love of bright eyes in the darkness of the depths of night. I show you that bright eyes and laughter are wonderful and magnetic. They draw people and ideas together.

➤ IMAGINATION TOOLS FROM THE MOON

- I show you bright eyes in the depths of the night. May they magnetize your ideas as they light your way.

- With bright eyes I also gift to you that you are powerful and magnetic when your smiles build to laughter.

- May your eyes magnetize your direction like a compass as you do the wonderful things you do with your ideas.

XIX The Sun

THE SUN indicates who you really are but maybe forgot when you were born. With a bright smile you reconcile opposites. You have your own inner light to illuminate the way on your journey. This will always come and go, ebb and flow, like sunlight. Remember, even if your inner light dims, it is soon to return like sunlight! Visualize both dawn and dusk. Feel their differences and THE SUN in between them. Feel the powerful changes that occur between the night and the day, and between the day and the night.

It is indicated that you see your inner light and shine as you feel the light of your natural truth and purpose. Shine brightly. Feel who you are. Refresh yourself inside and out! THE SUN card indicates that you experience your own glory as you respect what you have to offer. Honor and use your own gains. Feel your pleasures. Experience your triumphs. Reap your bright success!

This is a time where you are more visible. Your way is bright and right. This time can be felt in a way like THE TOWER card, minus the upheaval and destruction. Everything about your identity is new and clear and bright and shines. Visualize dawn and dusk. Feel the differences. Feel the powerful presence of your ideas that THE SUN highlights. Enjoy your vitality and health to brighten these areas.

It is indicated to be extra mindful here. Literally, do not trip yourself up or be blinded by your ideas. There is no

The Sun
Self, return, bright success

need to do that ever. There are forces here – be they objects, energy, and/or people – that you cannot see or of which you may not be aware. This will be similar to the 7 OF SWORDS. Open your eyes. Feel around for them. Shine your light on those things to your benefit.

THE SUN indicates that you deserve to shine. It also suggests that your brightness is more than an appearance. Shine with substance from within! Take yourself somewhere and brighten a new perspective. There, drop bad and old and outdated habits. Look to the different kind of light present in the visions of THE MOON. Feel sunlight directly as you imagine a connection to THE SUN. Shine in a new way! Shine IN a new way for yourself! You may feel more in sync with YOUR MOON. If so, adjust your pace. Your perspective will follow and reel out the night to draw the day into your imagination. YOUR SUN then syncs up with your smile and shines fully! Light up the breadth of your experiences here to prepare for what comes up next. Polish your magical scale! Get it ready!

Enter The Sun

Good morning, good evening. A great sunny day to you whenever you visit my bright place! You see I know no time. I always shine. It is simply your perspective that shifts me on that cool, big rock called Earth. It appears that I go away. I do go away. And, I am also always soon to return. Your earth spins AND circles around me. It is cool to have a dance partner like that in orbit around me. Earth is like one of your ideas to me. Remember that I shine for you even at night. You can say hi then if you want by simply bank-shotting your hello off THE MOON! I am another light that brightens your eyes. Smile inside and POOF I am there! Guess who taught me that?!

You see, as THE SUN I am who you were when you were born. You may not remember. You may have forgotten. Your identity is still wonderfully present, though. It does not leave you. I am the glow of your inner inheritances. I am your own treasure to discover. Your talents amaze me! Develop them as you see fit. You are the gardener of your soul! You will learn more about this with the 7 OF PENTACLES.

I am strong because I am subtle and constant. I simply shine no matter what. I shine even behind the clouds when you cannot see me. I am still there no matter what the weather, just like you. You may have storms now and then that cloud over me. Know that even when you feel like it is raining cats and dogs in your mind where tears flood through your eyes, I am still there. Breathe and weather your storms as your eyes are washed. They will shower you off and brighten you up for my return. Then, you can be refreshed and shine even brighter. I am there for you no matter what, 100 percent. Win, lose, or draw. I like how you rise to the occasion and shine with the things that you enjoy. Remember that anytime you feel perplexed, you can always try a new perspective. I suggest Yours. ☺ THEN, see your perspective from different angles and find what feels right. See your ideas in different lights.

I love to remember who I really am but forgot when I entered this life. I am still THE SUN. I am new every day. I love that even when you think I am gone, I will soon return each morning. Think of this to toss off worry. No news is good news from me. I will always be back. One hundred percent, remember? One hundred percent.

➣ *Imagination Tools* From The Sun

- I gift you a true, inner inheritance for you to discover and treasure. I gift you the true treasure of the inheritance you were born with. YOU! Discover your inner riches!

- I gift to you the Imagination Tool of being able to refresh yourself with a stretch like I do in the morning as I stretch and rise through the dawn.

As I come and go each day, keep your uniquely complete gifts refreshed and bright and treasured. Shine and rest and dream with actions as only YOU can!

XX Judgment

JUDGMENT indicates weightless memories in your mind that exact a heavy toll or simply take a lot of energy. They slow you to provide a breadth of self-born experience. JUDGMENT is the experience of everything natural and unseen underground that works to burst forth into the light! JUDGMENT does not indicate to hurry. It does indicate not to dig in your dirt so to speak. Wait patiently and respect your memories. In respectful remembrance forget them as you tend to your ideas. They will sprout and grow and flower on their own in time soon, when it is time.

It is indicated that you alone carry your memories into the present. You are no more at the mercy of your past than you are of old photo albums. Take more good pictures in your imagination! JUDGMENT indicates the respectful remembrance that perennials have as they poke their noses up in newly amended soil at their time in their season. This indicates a time where the cycles of your memories will flourish in your ideas. Tend your ideas as they surface on their own. Do not dig things up. Simply spruce up where they will be. Work with your memories as your dreams bring them to sprout and burst forth to enhance your ideas. To be at peace with your past is also indicated.

Judgment
Patience, respect, renewal

Enter Judgment

I would say hello, but I am a concept and not a thing. I would rather say SURPRISE! I am Judgment! I am about those things that have not yet arrived but are about to do so. I am like friends who are on their way to your birthday party. That is the kind of energy I would like to show you for your idea solar system. I would like to show you the garden of your imagination that always grows and develops and buds and blossoms. I am here for you to learn to notice these things daily as you enjoy them. I also would like you to learn to notice when a daily thing is a BIG HUGE NEW thing!

I embrace the weightless qualities of your memories in your mind that fuel your dreams. Sometimes memories may feel heavy and begin to take a lot of energy. These can also provide you with a way to experience your perspective differently as you adjust your pace. The heaviness can often be a cue that your whole idea solar system moves. Remember THE EMPEROR. His every step is heavy as he can adjust the pace and direction of his whole world with a single step. And, like THE HERMIT, his every step also refreshes his world.

I love to respect the past and leave buried memories buried. I respect that they are underground. Because of this I do not dig in my dirt and disturb their sleep. I let the seeds of memories sprout on their own. I enjoy it as they burst forth at their own pace! I love my dahlias, fern peonies, pansies, and tiger lilies. But, I never tell them to hurry. Glad, too. They would probably have a hoot of a laugh at me in good fun if I did. They might even get some woolly thyme to play a trick on me.

I love respectful remembrance. I love to forget things into memory. As I forget, new flowers sprout in new places. My garden is naturalized. The flowers of ideas often poke up their noses in fresh and new places. When things appear slow here, there is a lot going on in tiny and unseen places.

➢ IMAGINATION TOOLS
FROM JUDGMENT

- I gift you that YOU are the gardener of your soul and your body and your life. I gift you to take care of yourself as the gardener of your *mindbodybeautiful*! For this gift I give you anticipation to smile in patience as your ideas grow.
- I only accept and give good back like in a garden. Call this one a gift to learn how to amend your soil. Learn what rejuvenates you. Remember that gardeners do not often change the soil. They simply add more good soil on top and water it so it settles in to nourish their ground. This is called amending the soil. Keep yourself fresh to nourish your ideas as they burst forth. Your ideas are the living sprouts underground in the garden of your imagination. Do things you enjoy as you forget the wait!
- Find fun ways to use your anticipation and patience. This exercise may put you in places long enough to see new sprouts of other ideas.
- The dreams you make are always yours to realize.

OH! Some people like the British spell my name "Judgment" with an "e" in the middle. Look around and decide for yourself how you spell my name. That will be another eensy weensy sprout to tailor your voice and magic.

XXI The World

A complete cycle is indicated. THE WORLD indicates that you are right back where you started and this cycle of your journey is complete. Look to new and bigger dreams. See the world IN THE WORLD card! You are looking up here. The view is from within an obelisk. See through the top of the obelisk as a looking glass, a portal to another world. See as if you are inside the obelisk looking up through its top. See the point of its top right in front of you where the lines cross. Visualize this vanishing point perspective at the top as a portal to infinity. Flow through the looking glass of this doorway into your next cycle. Build on the foundation of this complete cycle.

THE WORLD indicates a powerful completion! A powerful cycle is complete along THE FOOL's journey. A powerful cycle is complete on your journey! You are right back where you started in a brand new, big way! A big cycle along your journey is now complete. Feel this complete cycle. Look to new and bigger dreams than before. Remember where you started. Feel the difference now.

THE WORLD card indicates an infinite outward dance. The fixed signs of the Zodiac in astrology provide constant and seamless links to this cycle. They integrate THE WORLD to the dynamic WHEEL OF FORTUNE. There are four signs here. There are four elements. There are four compass points.

The World
Complete cycles, expansive, infinite

There are four corners of the universe. The four fixed signs of Leo, Taurus, Aquarius, and Scorpio provide The World with a place for each of these points. The World is also symbolic of the All. All is within sight and all is within reach here.

The World indicates completion and wholeness with permanence and satisfaction and happiness. The World card indicates that everything has come together successfully. Dream more dreams and continue on your path. Circular branches form here. New cycles and scales link strongly and naturally with where you are now.

Look to all the cards, especially The Fool now on a new journey. Look to The Queen of Wands for energetic and clear vision. Adjust your pace and direction and perspective to work towards your new dreams. The World sprouted the epic spiral of giving and receiving that grew into the 6 of Pentacles. Imagine yourself as The Fool and be container and contained at one and the same time. You are a not a mystery here. Your current inner ideas are a whole world. Adjust your scenery. Re-arrange more than just one room. Clean house inside and out to prepare for your new dreams.

Enjoy this time and make a seamless segue into the next cycle of your journey!

Enter The World

Glad you have met all my Big-Place friends here in Mystereum! I am The World. I hold all of Mystereum and beyond! I include you and your imagination. The coolest thing to me is that I feel that YOU encompass all of ME, too!

There is a whole world in your imagination to link with. I am yours to explore and discover and dream and live your dreams into your life.

First, I would like you to settle in and spend some time and remember the gifts you have been given thus far in Mystereum. We thank you as you remember each *Imagination Tool*. We would all like you to think of a gift that you have received here or a gift that you have imagined that you already had. Any gift that pops into your mind is the one we look for you to see. We encourage you to write this gift down in your own personal notebook. Take many deep and strong breaths as you do.

You see, we feel you have what you need in the big picture of Mystereum. Maybe you start to feel that you had it all along. That is cool kewel stuff! Take this time to pause and notice the biggest cycle of all in your life that has come full circle. Was it a challenge? Was it a test? Is it something you made or worked to learn? Feel The Sun and The Moon from their perspectives from day to day and night to night. When you see The Moon during the day, watch it play with The Sun. Then, after you have let that settle in, we have a request. Feel The Sun and The Moon as they might feel on the DAY that a New Year begins as an exercise of thought. Feel The World in your world then.

We know there are many things going on all the time. Remember that your *Imagination Tools* are here to inform your journey and make it more vibrant. Remember to discover and strongly enhance the experiences you have. From here on out Mystereum is yours. Imagine and discover and share as you see fit. Remember when you wore your safety gear at THE TOWER and were asked to get ready to be the boss? POOF! Now, you are! It is your call where to go next. As we say here, "If you are having fun with an idea, you are using it even better than well." All the Best to You as you continue your journey of imagination and discovery! We are always here in *Archetypal Imagination* when you need us. Simply bring us to mind! We are honored to be here for you, and look forward to see where you take us next! Always a HOOT having more cool stuff to discover! Use your imagination to decide where to set out on your next journey . . . each time.

⇒ IMAGINATION TOOL
FROM THE WORLD

- I gift you the Imagination Tool of a thought. To master things does not mean you have no more to learn and experience from them. Mastery leads to further discovery. May your masteries fulfill your journey and your discoveries make it more vibrant. Play with the wonderful world of your imagination and celebrate your discoveries!

Oh, here is a souvenir before you giddy up and move on about! It is a bit of history about the obelisk in Mystereum. The view through the looking glass at the top of our obelisk has special meaning for Mystereum's ROYAL COURT. They see the top of the obelisk as a looking glass to see the infinite world of your next cycle. They also see the top of our obelisk as a powerful portal between worlds. You see, they feel it is also a connection to the afterlife that they use regularly each time they finish their large works. They call the top of the obelisk "The Portal of the Seamless Segue." They say that in each joyful completion of a cycle it gives you a glimpse of eternity.

I once heard the 4 ROYAL COURTS say, "Pyramids are themselves their own foundation. They are set on the sands of time." I felt that as I created and made the top of our obelisk as a portal.

Part Two

Grounding Imagination

The Fool's Journey Through Pentacles

The Ace of Pentacles

The ACE OF PENTACLES indicates ideas that will excite you to utilize your natural and wonderful and valuable assets and seeds! This is a place where your enthusiasm matters a great deal! Look at your room or desk or office or playground. When you are completing things, is the tide out? Are there shells all over the beach, so to speak? When you are just starting things, is the tide in? Are simply sand and water present? Is all clear and clean for fresh starts and finishes and celebrations for new ideas as you can see the subtle things? Have fun in this new time. Your creative seeds sprout underground before you see them burst into the sun!

Grow naturally from here. Even though you are different just like everyone else is different, you can provide THE most crucial difference with your ideas. It is indicated that your conditions are full of possibilities. Strengthen your connection to explore your brand of life. Share tokens or symbols of love and affection. Do not be afraid to get your hands dirty. Be messy. Your work, rather than the appearance of work, is important. You will know. That is enough. Have fun as things burst forth in this new time. Remember the sand on a beach. Wash off in the water as you feel ready to do so. New growth is really subtle. New growth can also be wonderfully messy like finger paints!

The Ace of Pentacles
Assets, seeds, new places

Enter The Ace of Pentacles

Glad you are here! You can see my portrait in the card. But, you just might not actually ever see me. I am one of those parts of Mystereum and your imagination that you feel in your heart. I present myself as really small. I am also so big and so *there* that you may miss me. The idea of a whole apple tree may be inside one of my seeds. Everyone here calls me Atman. I am larger than large. I am smaller than small.

I am your inner inheritances. I am wonderful qualities that you were born with! Learn to recognize me. I feel that natural gifts are always worth a pause and a look. Feel your natural gifts, what is in them, and the best way to proceed. Switch up your pace to feel and see more. This can be done even for several minutes. JUDGMENT is a great friend of mine! Like seeds and your inner inheritances I often first burst forth from unseen places. I am felt even when unseen in the underground goings on of your rich imagination. Do you feel any of those kinds of things now?

When everything looks pretty much the same and you see and feel and sense new feelings, I suggest you pause. In those moments, feel my personality as a small JUDGMENT card here, with a little HANGED MAN to accent me. JUDGMENT stops by to chat with me quite a lot. I have realized that I am Judgment, too. I simply live in a smaller world at a smaller scale. MINE! It is big enough for me. I excite new things to be fresh here!

Remember back to JUDGMENT where you were honored as the gardener of your own soul to see in to the underground where I operate. I ask for you to have a little patience with your imagination. Remember that a smile or two is like watering me. An ear to ear, bright smile with laughter adds the best fertilizer for me to grow in your ideas! I am here when you want to focus on new things that come into your imagination and your world. Do not hesitate to think me up. I may already be there. I like to pretend I am an apple tree even when I am simply a seed. Pretend is powerful a lot of the time! Pretend is especially powerful when you garden your soul! Your pretend is yours to use in your own, wise way!

Details here may be as soft as a whisper. Look closely, though. There may be plenty there that grows bigger than an apple or oak tree soon. I like to appear in Mystereum just after THE WORLD. Worlds are similar to what I make from a single seed. Stick around here. Feel how you can grow something from single idea!

⇒ *Imagination Tools*
From The Ace of Pentacles

- I gift you the ability to sense inner inheritances as they prepare to come to light.
- I gift you the idea to focus and tend ideas from their first sprout. You may become able to recognize them by their first leaves. With practice you may also be able to feel the seeds of ideas as they burst forth from your imagination.
- I gift you to recognize and forget bad habits to increase the potential of your ideas. This is a gift of attention to the power and beauty to nurture the proper details in your ideas, and the ones to come.
- I gift you to feel how to grow a whole idea solar system from a single idea.

I look forward to see you surprise yourself over and over with your ideas.

The 2 of Pentacles

The 2 of Pentacles indicates balance and to strive for equality. Do not choose instant gratification at the expense of your purpose. There is responsibility when you take on only what you can handle while you negotiate choices. It is indicated to be a thick time to make sure every idea performs its own balanced part. Keep only consequences in mind.

The 2 of Pentacles indicates that you have power in connections that balance. Strive for equanimity as you choose not to indulge in instant gratification. You are responsible for taking on only what you can handle. Keep your values in mind. Choice and negotiation are assets.

Do not let it be a hassle or a struggle to dance the fine line between your practical and sensual realities. Tactile pleasures, things you can touch, can put you in position to resolve practical issues. Roll up your sleeves and get to work. Get your hands dirty. You may have fun, and also put effective methods in place.

Be what is present as you balance yourself! Communicate your concrete issues, concerns, and ideas a great deal here. Bring them forth to balance yourself as you make connections. Be active as you even your keel.

Enter The 2 of Pentacles

The 2 of Pentacles
Balance, equality, detail

Hey there! We both welcome You! ☺☺ This is the place in Mystereum where ideas work together. Your ideas work together here at the smallest of scales. We connect and ground ideas here as we bring their first inklings together. Feel the fresh-from-their-inklings creation of your ideas and begin to connect them. A healthy start is in your imagination. Couple that with tangible things.

Long ago we found that we linked our ideas with the core of our imagination. It was like we plugged in to a never-ending energy source. We found that the influence of a single connection can cascade through the whole of our idea solar system. This makes the start of good habits with even the smallest of your ideas. Pair things strongly.

Everyone here calls us "The Watchmakers." The title fits. We work with hidden ideas. We keep them clean and polished. They take no more than they need. We connect ideas that fit and are effective together. They begin to touch upon and influence more things as they grow.

We love your balance and how you team up your ideas. We do not choose instant gratification as our purpose has too much value for that. We search for the most basic elements to make the core of our ideas real. We absolutely love values and a responsibility to work with only what we can handle. This leaves plenty of room for us to choose and negotiate with our ideas as important assets. We tune and tailor them as we go along. To tune and tailor along the way is our negotiation. This is important to our team. We make sure every idea does its part in balance as we keep consequences in mind.

THE CHARIOT comes here to relax and rejuvenate. He acts much like we do. He is simply much larger and faster. We dig that we are in similar lines of life.

➢ *IMAGINATION TOOLS*
FROM THE TWO OF PENTACLES

- We gift you a direct line from your feet to your imagination. Let yourself feel your own two feet clearly. Feel subtle things with your feet as you experience them.

- We give you the idea to feel your toes as little versions of your fingers. Ground-grabbers? Connect yourself to the ground as your instinct points your distinct way. You can see the whole world of an idea's potential in its smallest details with this.

- Our morning and evening workout is simply to feel and imagine things as soon as they touch our feet. Try it for yourself! Enjoy!

The 3 of Pentacles

The 3 OF PENTACLES indicates your industry, hard work, and talent pay off. Work on some sort of project with all of your talents. Utilize your mind and body and spirit. No one else thinks just the way you do! Be creative with your ideas. Express them to people you trust. A lot of what you are doing may have a greater significance than you realize. Feel that. Enjoy this time. You cannot lose another's race. Your joy touches lives with lasting impressions!

Use your creativity to enhance and reinforce what you already do. What do you do naturally that is wonderful? Ask others. They may help you realize what this is. Connect smiles to power orbits in your idea solar system as you as you bring your ideas to life right in front of you!

Enter The 3 of Pentacles

Come on in to our place where groups first form! We start out your 3s in motion on solid ground. You put things together in your imagination with 2s. Here, ideas will begin to move into groups and compositions where they work together. The 3 is the first number of a group. We begin to group very solid and earthly aspects for your journey.

We love your hard work where your talents pay off. We utilize all the talents we have. Our minds, bodies, and spirits

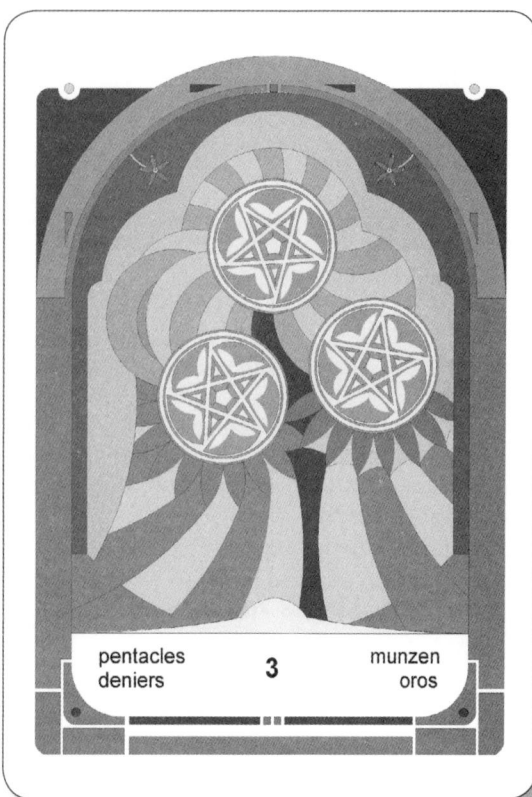

The 3 of Pentacles
Industry, hard work, groups

make a wonderful group. We do not feel that your ideas are common. No one else thinks just the way you do! Be creative as you discover what can be done with your ideas and express them to trustworthy people. It is cool to us that a lot of times we begin a project with our ideas that has a greater significance than we first thought. Take care to plan and know that this is your process. Win in your own special way. Our presence in a group is important to us. Our joy to group things together touches lives and leaves lasting impressions.

With three, we are careful not to move too fast. But, together can we turn on a dime. Any one of us can tug off in another direction in an instant. We work together to sense best which direction we want to take together as we enjoy lots of turns!

⇒ IMAGINATION TOOL
FROM THE THREE OF PENTACLES

- We gift you the tool to perceive positive groups that you can form with your ideas. You can use these to your advantage to bring your ideas to reality.

The 4 of Pentacles

The 4 OF PENTACLES indicates to strengthen your base. Foundations and support systems are the focus. Material stability and physical strength form abundance, security, and balance. Work to strengthen your body and things that make you feel secure. It is a positive time to take stock of the things around you and reinforce your foundation. Prepare and protect yourself. Plan for future lulls or downtimes and you may actually avoid them.

The 4 OF PENTACLES indicates that your world is supportive. Your material strength enhances your stability. Your power in any material form expresses your abundance. Strengthen your body to strengthen your castle. The power of your assets and to build things with your allowance is indicated. Feel how the material world is secure and stable. Notice the things around you. They are indicated to have very prominent assets.

Enter The 4 of Pentacles

Welcome to the place where your hidden supports are always present. You are in the place where the simple ground you stand on can be as inspirational as the stars in your sky! We ask that you remember JUDGMENT, but dig

The 4 of Pentacles
Foundations, support, physical strength

here. Respect the peace of hidden things that operate for you on their own. These hidden treasures are there to keep your ground magical. They will come to you as they do of their own accord as your inner inheritances develop. Now is a great time to simply enjoy where you are. Dig a little and raise your hands up high and stretch. You are right where you need to be!

We love to provide natural, hidden supports that strengthen the weight of the ideas you balance and measure and group in your world. We love you to be strong and stable. Power in any material form that is stable will enhance matters of abundance and security. A strong body is a great thing to focus on here.

Maybe the power of your allowance can be used to get something to enhance the castle you build in your imagination. Our place is all about your material world and the world around you. Bring security and stability here when you visit. Or, visit if you need some. You are in the place of a supportive material world here. Celebrate the magical ground all around you that is also right under your feet!

⇒ IMAGINATION TOOL
THE FOUR OF PENTACLES

- We gift you the tool of hidden supports that are always present to structure your imagination. May the ground be magical under every step!

The 5 of Pentacles

The 5 OF PENTACLES indicates physical and material trouble that can constrict your emotions. Look within yourself. Determine what must be changed to improve your situation. Is the trouble simply created by your perspective? Is the trouble created by an expectation? Do you miss your own warm and established inner light?

Do not be blind to the all the blessings around you. Your warm and established inner light may hide in plain sight behind clouds of uncertain expectations. This can cause you material distress. Do not transform negative thoughts. Forget them like wheat does chaff. It is simply blown off in the wind. Feel like a bird with a broken wing that has healed. Set yourself free to fly.

You are suggested to think, "All that's left is. . . ." and remember that Pandora found hope in the bottom of a box. She found hope after all the negative things left the box. This is a great time to transform limitations you feel. Move around expectations that cause you pain. Forget them.

The 5 OF PENTACLES can indicate physical and material trouble that cause feelings of loss. Look within and heal yourself from the inside, not from the edges. Amend your soil. Forgive yourself. Maybe this brings you a smile as you release these things. Forget them to get back your brightness. Do not feel sorry for yourself or separate yourself from the blessings all around you. If you are mad at yourself for some reason, change your gear with a walk. Simply do something else for a little bit. Let things clear up on their own time.

Beware of daydreams that substitute patterns and cloud your dreams. Think self-limitation. Become more aware of your soul. Gather strength and gain focus to develop your uniqueness. Value your life wonderfully and do not react to impulses. Take deep breaths as you act at this time to help settle the new balance that is in your mix. As soon as you decide on something, then take at least one deep breath and one big step. You may feel like you are on rock bottom. Change your perspective. Move to another place with a big breath and a step. Literally change your perspective. Rock bottom is also a strong place to stand. Strong as a rock. Stand up tall on a hard surface with your arms raised and breathe deeply.

Enter The 5 of Pentacles

Just to let you know, mind your footing here. This is another step-by-step place. Once you receive it, we suggest that you have your 3 OF SWORDS Imagination Tool ready to use here. See and feel the bright core of what really goes on in your situation when we arrive. Go ahead and skip forward to receive the 3 OF SWORDS Imagination Tool and then come on back. No hurry. Mind your footing.

We find that flow is most important here. Emotions can often increase that flow. There can be a tangible strength of release in tears. Consider them an inner storm, your inner weather. With the right tools you can wash up with yourself

The 5 of Pentacles
Expectation, emotions, release

on your beach after the storm has broken. Tears can mingle with your lake. Your ACE OF CUPS will cleanse them from there. You can jump forward to receive from the ACE OF CUPS, too! You have done your job when you release painful structures you are simply comfortable with out of habit and expectation. Maybe you do not need some things any more. We recommend to not reason with the things you release. Simply release them.

We like you to see your warm, inner light glow like your own, personal sunlight. You can have a sun that shines even through the heaviest of tears. This light is yours. Sense it and be aware of its glow as it flows. We embrace physical and material crises here. So, give your light the strength to glow through thick and thin. We suggest not to focus on loss. Focus to embrace discomforts. They may be ready to release. Release them fully if so. Use your ACE OF CUPS and 4 OF PENTACLES Imagination Tools here.

This place in Mystereum is about the warmth and love you feel as you look within at tough times. Here you can feel what to change. Improve your situation with a powerful release. A lot of gardening goes on here. We weed to help your magical ground breath clearly. That is top priority here.

We learn how to forgive ourselves and others. Begin to love to utilize your creativity to rise above limitations. Honor and be considerate to exactly what really goes on here. Your garden may already have a rosy picture you do not see. No need to paint one. See it!

⇒ *IMAGINATION TOOLS* FROM THE FIVE OF PENTACLES

- We give you a tool to feel your imagination as a warm and established inner light. You can use this to assist you to release things that do not work for you anymore. We suggest that you bless yourself as you release them.

- Forgetting can be for getting. It will make more room for good.

The 6 of Pentacles

The 6 OF PENTACLES indicates to give and receive in life's epic spiral. Honest and substantial communication with a mutual exchange breeds justice here. Feel the power of an everyday devotion. Powerfully witness yourself connect and be connected with. This is a place of a circular branch where no one loses! Enjoy this confident and wonderful place where you get what you give and give what you get!

To give and receive in life's epic spiral is not charity here. JUSTICE is present in reciprocality. With an everyday devotion communicate with honesty and a powerful witness of the things you love.

Visualize to give and receive as a vast spiral that is part of your life. This is JUSTICE at play. Do what is natural and you can care for one another in both times of hardship and times of plenty. We give what we get. We get what we give. It is a circle where no one loses, a circular branch that gives and receives at all scales and in every direction. Feel this kind of mutual exchange in your idea solar system.

Enter The 6 of Pentacles

Hey there! As you look into this part of Mystereum you are looking upward! We live up here in the sky! THE HIGH

The 6 of Pentacles
Epic spiral, mutual exchange, circular branch

PRIESTESS gave you an ability to give form to the formless. We are two smaller versions of her. We keep all the things you form fresh by movement. We juggle them back and forth! It is a fun game of two-way catch to keep all your ideas moving naturally like planets! You simply need to focus on the ideas you have at hand. We will mind the orbits of your other ideas until you get back to them. Know they are always up here in the sky of your imagination. Toss us your focus and join the game!

We juggle-toss-play as we give and receive back and forth to each other in the epic spiral of your ideas. There is only honest communication here. We move ideas back and forth to keep their motions balanced. We like to think of ourselves together as mercurial. There is another word for a field trip for you! ☺ Look up "mercurial." It is pretty simple on the surface. We are as agile with our moods as we are in our motions. We know how to juggle each idea with rest and play. This way each idea has its own place or orbit in your idea solar system. Think of us across the whole solar system of ideas in your imagination. There will always be reciprocal work going on there. Look for partners to play with your ideas.

We also suggest that there is a power when you have an everyday devotion to your ideas. Powerfully feel your ideas daily. Powerfully witness and acknowledge them up here even if you simply direct an intent smile as you walk by or enjoy a picnic. Your daily awareness of your ideas will help us keep your imagination fresh so it can move with good balance. We dig our job!

Feel free to add and edit and tune and tailor your ideas here. For the idea solar system of your imagination we suggest to think of a circular branch. It goes round and round all the while branching about. This can paint a picture for you of our epic spiral. You cannot lose here. Balance your ideas in a fun way like a game!

➔ IMAGINATION TOOL
FROM THE SIX OF PENTACLES

- We gift you the tool of orbits for your ideas in your idea solar system. May you orbit your ideas as you feel best!

The 7 of Pentacles

The 7 OF PENTACLES indicates that your hard work has been done and it is a time for quiet watchfulness. Pause as your ideas gestate to develop all of their parts. Your work magnetizes your ideas. Realize that tangible material success in some form is indicated to be on its way. Take this time of powerful inner witness to visualize wonderful outcomes for your ideas. Let them simply arrive as they do. You may have other areas of your idea solar system to tend.

It is also indicated not to become attached to the outcomes you visualize here. Simply gaze upon the soulful garden of your imagination. Smile as you become attached to being delightfully surprised! This is a fantastic place to use your time wisely. Be active and invigorated in your other endeavors. Let your primary focus settle in and grow on its own!

Enter The 7 of Pentacles

Feel the float here! That is not the sky behind your fertile and abundantly fruiting plant. That is the sky BELOW your plant! You have transcended the solar system of your 6s. Here your solar system can ALL be in that one plant AND be all around and below you, too. Maybe you are the gardener of

The 7 of Pentacles
Quiet watchfulness, pause, above

your soul and this is the place where you do that. Your whole imagination and more is here above everything.

We suggest that you are in a place where you are able to be truly aware of the strength and depth at the height of your ideas. Your ideas have developed and will soon bear fruit! You are developed so deeply here that you are placed in a depth that is ABOVE. This is a sacred place inside you for your imagination to expand as you pause and reflect. Here your thoughts and ideas can be within you, in front of you, and all around you all at one and the same time!

Feel back to THE HANGED MAN with you AS the tree. See him from above with you also AS THE HANGED MAN at the same time. Your hard work has been done and your idea solar system now has wonderful orbits! Enjoy this time as you quietly watch your ideas come to more fully develop. They expand further possibilities here!

We suggest not to concern yourself with material success here. It comes naturally from here. Reflect on wonderful outcomes for your ideas to prepare yourself for the work to come. This reflection can rest and refresh you. Reflect in the soulful calm that is here above everything. Let things come as they may. You will be able to keep track of everything in orbit and how things work together soon enough. You may smile for no reason here. We often do. Let your smiles pulse like a heartbeat to give your ideas further life. You may start to feel more and more possibilities! Enjoy the commencement here. There is a mastery in soulful pause. Feel to your further discoveries. Reflect. Simply reflect. Use your time wisely in quiet watchfulness! Feel your imagination expand here as you reflect.

⇒ *IMAGINATION TOOL*
FROM THE SEVEN OF PENTACLES

- We gift you a place above everything for your imagination to expand. This is a place where you can see and feel all of the wonderful possibilities of your ideas expand.

The 8 of Pentacles

The 8 OF PENTACLES indicates that you have arrived at a beautiful plateau in your work. This is a natural and ordered place where you can see how things have come together. Support and direct your further growth from here. This place is much like an upper base camp in your creative process. Your intentions are often over-rated here. From here on, intention and meaning are better suited to occur in your creative actions. This is a place where it is simply far more important the way things come across. There is a very present glimpse of all directions from this vantage point. Know that if you feel depletion in certain areas, it may indicate misspent efforts there. Notice those places. You have full-on project support for labors of love in the right places. They are best suited to the energies here.

The 8 OF PENTACLES further indicates to support and direct your growth and the growth of your ideas. It is suggested to focus on satisfaction with your work and the things you will do with it. You do not need to perfect yourself here. Remember your inner inheritances. The meaning of your work occurs in the very act as you do it. Your ideas are abundantly gifted. A sense of fulfillment is at the core of the 8 OF PENTACLES.

Expand your means and resources within your means and resources. Your work is best suited to you in this place when it is a labor of love. Amend your imaginative soil with deep breaths. Your solid foundation here does not have mis-

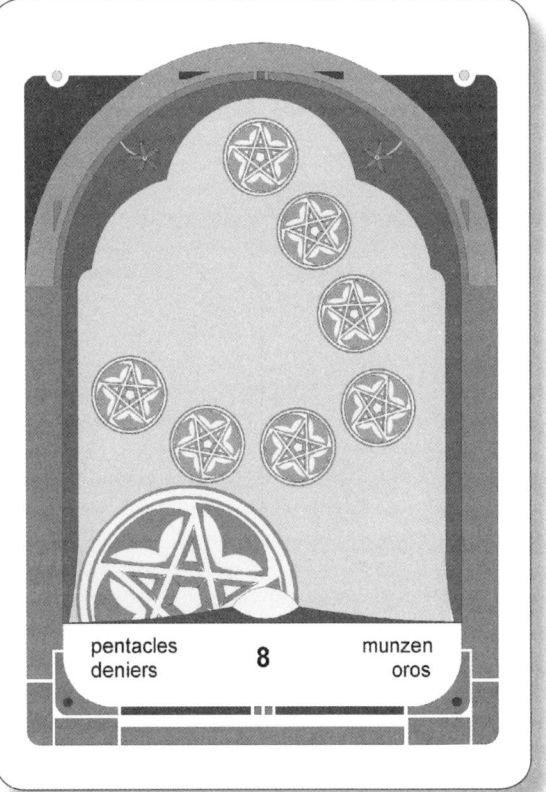

The 8 of Pentacles
Exquisite, a completion point

spent efforts. It gives you something to brace against and feel your effective progress.

Enter The 8 of Pentacles

Feel your possibilities flow from your expansive imagination! Sense the orange and gold together here. Orange is for your sacral chakra. It is the domain of your hips. They are the part of your agile base where your actions originate. This is a wonderful example of the idea of a strong and agile foundation. The waist. Feel your Waist-Power!

Gold is for your crown chakra. It is the domain of the top of your head where your spirit continuously meets your imagination and flows into and from your body. Our 8 body is a temple to us. May your body be a temple, too! To us the gold crown chakra is the portal of the spirit into your body. Feel your whole body as it works together and your possibilities pour in and out in an abundant dance-flow!

Here we support and direct growth with satisfaction in our actions. Make sure the things you do satisfy you. There is no need to be perfect. Your fully formed ideas are ready to pour forth from your imagination. Incorporate and develop them further right in front of you. Nourish your insides as your ideas nurture the things you love around you! Here all meaning occurs in the act.

Naturally place labors of love. They cause no depletion. Which ideas in front of you are NOW best suited to your energies? Which new things will provide solid foundations?

Pick your best ideas now right in front of you. Respect them as you do your dreams. Your dreams can begin to become real outside now. You are their foundation. Brace them against you as you move forward with your dreams. You have a ways to go from here, but abundant gifts grow here to be utilized fully.

⇒ *Imagination Tools*
From The Eight of Pentacles

- We gift you the tool of another portal. This is another doorway. Bring your ideas through it to get them right in front of you to develop them further! You decide which part of us will be your new doorway.

- We also gift you a fun perspective. The 8 is like the infinity symbol ∞ turned. We think that is pretty cool! Two complete 4s pair up to make our 8, and it rotates to expand as ∞

The 9 of Pentacles

The 9 OF PENTACLES indicates a certain level of success where you have an ability to appreciate the good things in life. The freedom to enjoy the fruits of your labors suggests to live your life with more freedom. Live on your own terms. Be free to explore your deepest desires. Also indicated is to go after real wants as you appreciate the simple pleasures in your life.

The 9s in general also carry an across-the-board dynamic in their balance. They have an order that is unique from other numbers. Feel material things that move towards completion. Keep reading to see the 9s gymnastic balance and order as you enjoy this invigorated time of personal freedom and happiness. Smile at the gratification your wonderful attitude brings as your best asset!

Enter The 9 of Pentacles

Welcome to our earthly 9s in the suit of PENTACLES! Think of PENTACLES as the earth working together with itself naturally all on its own always. That is like us! We are our favorite number! It may appear that there are a lot of us here. But, we overlap our multiple perspectives like a mirror makes two of you. One looks the other way back into you. It does this from you. That is the magic of the mirror!

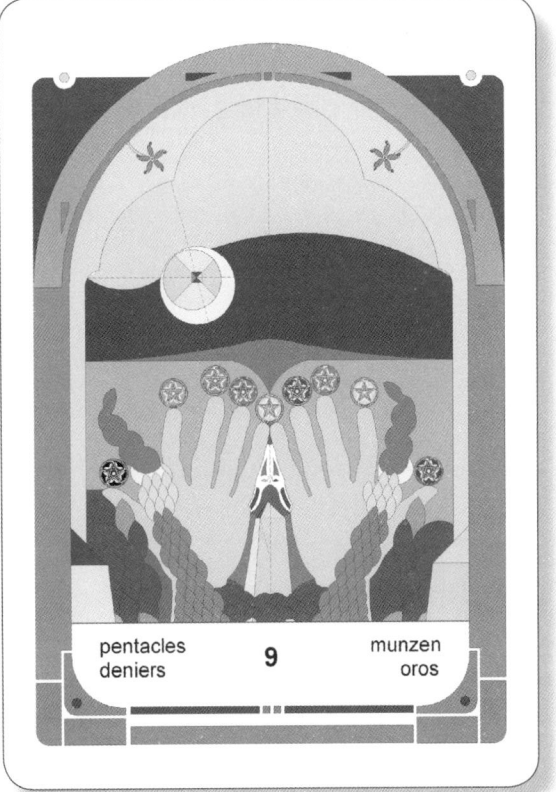

The 9 of Pentacles
Overlaps, finery, naturalized

There is really simply one thing. The mirror expands your perspective to do more than one thing can. Mirrors reflect and expand perspective. Again, it may appear that there are a lot of us here. Really there are more. Also less. We feel that when our identities work together AND are all versatile, it in fact takes less to create a more vibrant scene. And, vibrant things certainly have more!

Check out how our multiplication table makes a uniquely balanced mirror! No other number quite folds over itself with a perfect fit like we do. Here goes our 9s and how they live in our multiplication table:

    09 18 27 36 45 54 63 72 81 90. See anything across the board?

Let us show you ourselves another way:

    09 18 27 36 45
    90 81 72 63 54, and go back to the original to see this another way:
    09 18 27 36 45 :: 54 63 72 81 90

See our mirror in the middle and how we can put all of us into two smaller groups that mirror-match each other AND are also unique and balanced at the same time? That is like two of you with a mirror. Both are similar. Each is unique. Magical! Mirrors make cool, real-time pretend for us.

Look closely at your smallest fingers, your pinkies. Touch them together as you look into our world here like we do. These are your hands that reach into our world. Reach through the portal of the border into our card. We can overlap and connect with you at the smallest places. That is our strength. We quickly become one group and just as quickly move apart into two coordinated groups. We can do this when we have wonderful communication with each other. Our right hand knows what our left is doing.

Now for some fun with your mirror. This is another, quick field trip for some fun. Find a big, polished metal kitchen spoon. Look at your reflection. Is it upside down or right side up? Now turn it around and POOF the curved mirror gives you another perspective and you did not change at all! Flip it around again. Flip it around. Fun, huh?! That takes our mirror another step to show you something. Sometimes you change one quality and POOF! You may see more than meets the eye, like here with our multiplication table!

➢ *IMAGINATION TOOL*
FROM THE NINE OF PENTACLES

- We gift you the tool to be able to sense just the right number of things in your idea solar system when you create things so that your ideas work together wonderfully. Feel this and it is so!

The 10 of Pentacles

The 10 OF PENTACLES indicates your prosperity and your close relationships. To share your inner inheritances is also indicated. Feel how contagious your smile is! Practical stability and the tangible, material, physical world are signified by the PENTACLE symbol. The true meaning of this card is found intuitively each time it appears. Your intuition is well grounded here to infuse your imagination with vibrancy. Meld your close relationships with your prosperity. Enjoy this time of bountiful ties and enrichment.

Remember that sometimes a surprise inheritance is something you discover that you already have.

Enter The 10 of Pentacles

Welcome to a point of completion. We are the 10 OF PENTACLES. We would like to let you know about the other tens, too. We will start with 10s in general. We have all grown from there. When you are placed with 10s you have come to the completion of a cycle. Remember your tools from THE WHEEL. THE WHEEL is a really big 10!

Similarities and differences have been expressed along your way from each of your friends in Mystereum. Some have been expressed from the perspective of their number. Some have been expressed from the perspective of their suit.

The 10 of Pentacles
Prosperity, close relationships, sharing

PENTACLES. CUPS. WANDS. SWORDS. THE MAJORS gave you large and rockin' places to experience!

You may discover that with Mystereum's 10s we have each developed a unique and complete identity. We each express our places in our own ways. So I do not crash any surprises, I will stop there. The other 10s will introduce themselves to you in their way. Enjoy working with all of us as you move towards your next cycle here. It is THE HIGHER COURT. After our 10s, you will be elevated into THE HIGHER COURT where the PAGES, KNIGHTS, QUEENS, and KINGS live! They are the place of your Higher Self. From what we have heard from your travels thus far, we feel that you will feel right at home there!

The 10s like to stand and deliver strongly. We prepare you for the fanfare of YOUR ROYAL COURT! Here in the 10 OF PENTACLES we love prosperity and close relationships. Inner inheritances and the sacred qualities you were born with drive our actions. We love practical stability in action. The tangible, material, and physical world is your oyster.

Grasp and embrace ideas and places that are right in front of you. How your ideas are presented is the utmost with us. We love to feel truth in a mountain or a river. We feel truth in a fire. We feel truth in the wind. We also feel it in substantial conversation it seems to have all these things. We love it when we discover things with our intuition and then discover them right in front of us. We love to feel the newness of solid things each time we experience them.

Remember the favorite places you go. THE TOWER expressed to you how ponds turn over. Here, visualize your favorite fishing hole. Visualize that wonderful place you go that gives back to you.

We love to meld close relationships with solid bases that mirror our inner inheritances. We LOVE inner inheritances! We especially love the inner inheritances that YOU were born with! Appreciate the ties and enrichment we bring. They make our neck of the woods in Mystereum go 'round.

➣ *IMAGINATION TOOLS* FROM THE TEN OF PENTACLES

- We gift you a tool to enhance and reinforce and strengthen your sense of fresh and new perspectives each time you encounter something. This tool is simply your ability to do so. Use it to create with the other talents you have.

- I gift you the simplest of ways to view YOUR 4 ROYAL COURTS in Mystereum. This is in no way everything about YOUR ROYAL COURT. This is a first step kind of idea to open the door to YOUR ROYAL COURT. Each ROYAL COURT has a PAGE, a KNIGHT, a QUEEN, and a KING. Your PAGES will bring new things in for you. Your KNIGHTS will help you incorporate these things. Your QUEENS help to evaluate them with their natural leadership. Your KINGS have them in place to implement. Enjoy this simple explanation as an Imagination Tool as you take your first steps into YOUR ROYAL COURT.

The Page of Pentacles

The PAGE OF PENTACLES indicates that your identity develops in a tangible way from new energies of the earth brought in by your well-grounded senses in the 10 OF PENTACLES. These new energies nourish your ground like a treasure ship's hull as it returns from a long voyage. With these new energies tune and tailor and play with your ideas as you see fit. Find new spaces to create and play as you grow. Also, spruce up the places you have. This is a time to begin in earnest to find the roots of what works for you. Look at yourself and your friends and your money and your health. Be studious and considerate while you tinker with things at length to see how they work. Tinkering is a great activity at this time.

Sense your placement and how things inhabit the world they live in around you at this time of new discoveries! Feel your identity develop further as you teach yourself new things that nourish your world. The PAGE OF PENTACLES is a royal person who is very studious and conscientious about money and respectful of others and their property. PAGES are often also playful. Play can nourish your discipline. You can even hide expert skill in play like a lion does. Tinker with things at length with this mindset to explore how they work. Work to understand how your ideas and their aspects and surroundings inhabit the world they live in. They can inform the placement of your ideas. Remember that PAGES often bring

The Page of Pentacles
New growth, treasures, solid discoveries

in new vibrancies to YOUR ROYAL COURT. This is the HIGHER COURT OF YOU. It is the domain of your imagination. Have fun and simply flow while you are active and develop your ideas. Look to the vitality in the community of your ideas to make new and solid connections.

Enter The Page of Pentacles

Welcome to YOUR ROYAL COURT. This is the place of your own divine royalty. Some call it your Higher Self. We welcome you and all of the light of your ideas that you bring for us to shine through Your Land of Mystereum!

I AM The PAGE OF PENTACLES

I love to help you tune and tailor the ideas you develop and bring into YOUR ROYAL COURT.

I love to grow and find new spaces for the ideas you discover and create.

I love to make new places for the solid strength of your creative work.

I love to send word through YOUR ROYAL COURT to tell of the new connections you have built under your dreams.

I love to discern the roots of what works with your inner riches. Your money, your health, and your studious and playful discipline show me how conscientious you are with no need of explanation. The work you incorporate from your inner riches makes that clear.

I love being considerate of others and their property.

I love how your ideas inhabit your world and thrive with their surroundings

⇒ *IMAGINATION TOOLS* FROM THE PAGE OF PENTACLES

- I gift you a tool to bring forth your discoveries. This tool is to group THE MAGICIAN, THE HIEROPHANT, and THE CHARIOT together to help present solid, new ideas. When you ride at speed into YOUR ROYAL COURT with this group, magical renewal is at hand!

- Take a field trip to explore Marco Polo. I would like you to make an Imagination Tool for yourself from your voyage. Have a blast!

The Knight of Pentacles

The KNIGHT OF PENTACLES indicates to incorporate earthbound goals. Here is your place to be consistent and steady as you apply your highest aspects. Work with diligence as you full-on feel your tasks AS the meaning. This is a place where meaning simply occurs in the act. This is what we mean in Mystereum when we express that reasons are often unreasonable. We certainly do not mean not to have any.

It is indicated to be very present with your actions at this time. Reasons may go wonderfully missing while you get things done. Have a spirited and active blast with your mundane, every day devotions!

This is the card of the joy of getting "lost" on a walk or run, in/on a kayak in the middle of a bay or in the ocean. "Lost" here indicates freedom from worry as you travel with intent and are only conscious of travel and exploration and discovery. "Lost" here indicates to experience the moment and breathe it in. Feel the concepts of loss and lost here to indicate freedom rather than no direction.

The KNIGHTS carry a natural sense of pride. Pride with the KNIGHTS is a combination of majestic victory and shining glory! This pride indicates to feel prominent and present in one's body within the environment. Reason is literally lost or shed and forgotten into right actions that are natural. This character indicates a full *mindbodybeautiful* presence

The Knight of Pentacles
Consistent, steady, diligent

with the justice of strength simply present. Imagine a lion with cubs frolic-stumble-rolling over its paws and its un-interfering glance and inner smile. This is the character of the youthful silverback. The KNIGHT OF PENTACLES often pictures THE HANGED MAN afloat in his clarity. There is a natural correspondence between the KNIGHT OF PENTACLES and THE HANGED MAN from different scales. Remember your JUSTICE Imagination Tools here. Look to THE HANGED MAN and the ways your KNIGHT OF PENTACLES incorporates new things that are brought in by the PAGE to YOUR ROYAL COURT.

Enter The Knight of Pentacles

I AM the KNIGHT OF PENTACLES.

I am consistent and steady as I apply my highest aspects. I weave my earthbound goals and expand my core from the inside.

I love to work with diligence, and full-on feel my task at hand AS the meaning. I connect light to dark and dark to light across my Fabric at the level of the ground. *Continuous* is a favorite word of mine with light and dark. Remember dawn and twilight.

I love to be present in my body in situations I value and cherish. I get comfortably "lost" in them. I love this as an active and present meditation of positive loss. I love to listen to a friend weave out a wonderful and long story that is a current part of their life.

I love to bounce-kelp as I feel currents ripple through me like when I am on a kayak. It is my seahorse that I use between lands. It feels like a friend's voice. Quiet and slow I bounce-kelp near a friend on the bay. My idea solar system is over the water. To look at the sky is enough for me there. I realize that wisdom begins young and is developed. I realize that my whole world can travel.

➢ *IMAGINATION TOOL*
FROM THE KNIGHT OF PENTACLES

- I gift you a tool to incorporate your discoveries into the fabric of your idea solar system alongside YOUR CHARIOT and YOUR HANGED MAN. May your discoveries form a beautiful tapestry to warm you as you incorporate more breadth into your idea solar system. Incorporate things at your own speed. Invigorate YOUR ROYAL COURT with a powerful silence that, like the earth, is both active and alive.

The Queen of Pentacles

The QUEEN OF PENTACLES indicates practical and down-to-earth qualities that are naturally present. She has a love of enthusiasm and encourages friends and family to exercise and take good care of their health. Feel nourished with benefits as you care for others and lead by example.

There is an intrinsic knowledge here that water conforms to its cup. From that there is a natural discipline to always keep the cup clean. Further, the right sized cup that is attractive and distinct is all she ever uses. She values the exquisiteness of distinct identities and she arranges chores to fetch wood and carry water so the home fire will light up big smiles. This is a time of wonderful companionship with the earth and those around you. Make sure the discipline of the ritual of your chores comes from your core.

The QUEEN OF PENTACLES may own a successful business. She nourishes her work and promotes everyone she cares about to have the utmost care. She does not see any problem with the idea to buy a kid a Steinway piano so they can make themselves into their own brand of Mozart. She knows all too well the far-reaching inner and outer merits of a good environment. The obvious may not be her focus.

This queen also indicates that you may even cherish a vehicle, or simply a well-designed dashboard in a convertible as important if you drive a bunch. Simply put, she feels that

The Queen of Pentacles
Practical, down to earth, nourishing

if something is going to be in your presence, it is best for it to be attractive and distinct. Exquisite is a staple thing to her. She will show you that beauty has a positive usefulness. She requires beauty in her environment. Even in silence, a tasteful enthusiasm is indicated. Tasteful is a great word for you with the QUEEN OF PENTACLES.

Enter The Queen of Pentacles

I AM the QUEEN OF PENTACLES. To be practical and down to earth are two of my loves.

I am enthusiastic and encourage my friends and family to exercise. I nourish things when I promote them to value and take care of themselves in ways only they are able.

I feel that water conforms to its cup. I feel that the cup must always be kept clean, be the right size for its contents, be attractive and distinct in its own right, and be respected back to its proper place when it is not in use. This is important for the home.

Exquisite things are the best things!

Love your everyday devotions as exquisite things. Do your chores. Fetch wood and carry water as you need. If you never carry too much, you will never hurry or strain your strength. I feel to carry too much is bluster. It is called a lazy-man's-load. That is unacceptable here.

Judgment made my exquisite throne in its image as my first garden began to sprout.

With care and attention to all of this done well, your home fire will always be exquisite and warm your ideas.

⇒ IMAGINATION TOOL
FROM THE QUEEN OF PENTACLES

- I gift you the tool of a vibrant, inner garden for the hearth and home fire in your imagination. May you nourish and tend all the things you value. May you celebrate YOUR ROYAL COURT as an exquisite place through all of your years!

The King of Pentacles

The KING OF PENTACLES indicates the Master Builder. He builds concrete and psychic structures together. He creates things with strong roots that live of their own accord. Things that stand the test of time are also indicated. Consider only things of quality here and fill your life with direct gestures. This is a place of grand and exquisite strength and wit. Structures here have clean lines that are spare of ornament. This is not the domain of the glorious. This is a place of grand simplicity. Visualize your body as a structure with clean lines that is spare of ornament. Nothing is extra.

This is the character who concretely builds dreams. Proper reinforcement is not a requirement. It is the norm. All exceeds expectations here. Formwork for the foundations has already been sloughed off. It is a forgotten memory. The foundations are strong inside and out. Internal reinforcement enhances and strengthens the base of structures. It is integral in them. This is the card of developed roots. Healthy and prominent accomplishments lead to further developments. Quick fixes here make for shallow roots

The King of Pentacles
Master Builder, stunning qualities

Enter The King of Pentacles

I AM the King of Pentacles.

I am a Master Builder.

I build concrete and psychic structures together. They stand the test of time as they live of their own accord. They have a very good connection to the ground with strong roots.

There is a glory when you express grand and exquisite ideas with strength and wit and directness in every gesture.

Never compromise quality.

I love to breathe in vibrant spaces that feel alive.

Make your ideas exquisite. Enhance, reinforce, and strengthen them in places for exquisite people, exquisite things, and further exquisite ideas.

The shortest distance between any two things in the kingdom is laughter. It may be the quickest way to bring everyone together, too.

Learn as you laugh. Laugh as you learn.

⇒ *Imagination Tool* From The King of Pentacles

- I gift you the totality of the place of Your Royal Court. May you keep it solid and exquisite. Increase its strength as you expand yourself with new discoveries. From here you can fly as high as your roots go deep.

These are the things I wish for you.

Part Three

Fulfilling Imagination

The Fool's Journey Through Cups

The Ace of Cups

The ACE OF CUPS indicates to open up to love and begin new things in your life. The psychic and spiritual realms are also indicated. Trust your intuition and receive the blessing of psychic messages. They nurture your love and restore your joy. Celebrate this time when your cup is full of goodness! Only add good things to your mix. The rest? Simply let them rest. Initiate your emotional and intuitive cycles to nurture love and restore joy. Your cup here is filled with dreams, visions, and inspirations welling up from within. Share them. Put your headphones on and take a great walk!

Enter The Ace of Cups

Jump on in! The water is great! I always pour clean, new water from my never-ending cup into this great lake. It gets used for all of the things that begin here in the Land of Mystereum. Swim around and hang out with me for a while. I do not get tired as I always hold this cup. In fact, it is really a cool fountain I had made to do the job. THE HIEROPHANT lent me his portrait to work with. I am really all the newness that flows through the waters of fulfillment here. Enjoy! Let your play refresh you!

I love to be open to love and new life. The psychic and spiritual realms are where I work the most. I trust my

The Ace of Cups
Trust intuition, nurture love, fresh ideas

intuition so I receive the blessings of my psychic messages. My imaginations, my intuitions, and my full thoughts flow as newness throughout Mystereum.

I keep things light and fresh as I keep my insides clean. When I simply keep things light and fresh, my work almost performs itself. I cannot remember the last time it felt like work. Maybe I work like a lion with expert skill masked in play. Maybe I simply enjoy myself as I flow around and make sure everything is fresh and ready for you here. I feel that is a wonderful job!

Glad you could make it! I feel that to enjoy yourself makes your work brighter for you and for everybody else, too!

⇒ IMAGINATION TOOLS
FROM THE ACE OF CUPS

- I gift you bright eyes to trust and flow through your ideas. Bright eyes and wide, ear to ear, grins. They present fresh things that rejuvenate things you already have. You may already know this.
- Smile when you feel fresh ideas at play in your imagination. Begin to express them.

The 2 of Cups

The 2 OF CUPS indicates that love and friendship heal and bring contentment. Relationships, harmony, and cooperation that satisfy you are also indicated. Feel how two things that join up and fill together are more than just two ones. With attraction present your feelings, your heart's desire, and your expressions trump being right.

There is a distinction made in Mystereum between being joined and united versus union. Two identities that feel mutual respect provide powerful witness and participate with one another. Feel the differences between things joined and between things in union. This is a Mystereum perspective. Union would be two identities that melt into one another. This feels muddy, like an average. Union feels to average them both and reduce the individual strengths they bring. Union feels to settle and erode things. To join together is different, though. It makes for interdependence. Each contributes in a mutual celebration of their individual uniqueness as they strongly connect.

Enter The 2 of Cups

Great to see you here in Mystereum where love and friendship heal. We love contentment, relationships that satisfy, harmony, and cooperation. They flow to fill and exchange

The 2 of Cups
Satisfaction, heart's desire, expressions

strengths. We join together to share and contribute to mutual fulfillment. We mix new and excited things together.

Here we find that two joined are more than simply two ones. Here your heart's desire is felt and can be seen in every feeling and expression and action you have. Here your feelings trump being right. Trust your feelings here. They are yours. Flow and share as you please.

You see, here in the 2 OF CUPS we are a baby TEMPERANCE. We are not at all about union. In fact, we find it a little creepy for things to average themselves out together. They mix-muddy away their identities that brought them together in the first place. We find the strength of two identities that celebrate each other and work well together make a better flow of energy.

We talk to TEMPERANCE quite a bit. Before we do, though, we often have a chat with the 6 OF PENTACLES to make sure we are refreshed. Then TEMPERANCE can better refresh our clarity to bring identities to celebrate together. You may find that there are identities of people, identities of places, and identities of things. Feel the places between them where they connect like with your 9 OF PENTACLES pinkies. The connections themselves have identities, too! The places in between are important to us.

Your ideas have identities, too! Feel how you pair up ideas and begin to group them in your idea solar system like the sun and the earth, like the earth and the moon. Celebrate them as you develop your ideas in your imagination. Fill your cups with wonderful creative energy.

⇒ *Imagination Tool*
From The Two of Cups

- We gift you another big, bright-eyed smile when you think of your identity and the character of your imagination. You bring it to every situation. Love yourself. Love your identity. Love your imagination. Celebrate it! This can help you make even tricky situations more clear. It also makes the strong situations you are in fulfill everyone more.

The 3 of Cups

The 3 of Cups indicates a feeling of celebratory fulfillment while working with someone or in a group. Personal growth is experienced here when you develop your friendships with celebration and enjoyable activities. Partnerships are also indicated. Notice how trees help each other stay strong and healthy when they grow in groups. Each tree's roots grow subtly different than the next so they work together and support the group. Each tree can grow as high as its roots grow deep. Trees support each other from underground when they grow together in groups

Enter The 3 of Cups

WOO HOO! Celebrate! Our cups are full and we like to dance around together with enthusiasm! Join us if you want! We dance more than we talk. It is our way! Dance to express all the things that are active and work in your play!

We love to feel full as we work with another who is just as enthusiastic. We love to work together within an active group. Wallflowers here are simply on the wallpaper. Everyone joins in here to get the party started. We ask that you toot your own horn here. Somebody has to start the band!

We love that our brand of personal growth is felt in motion and dance. We celebrate as we develop the friendships

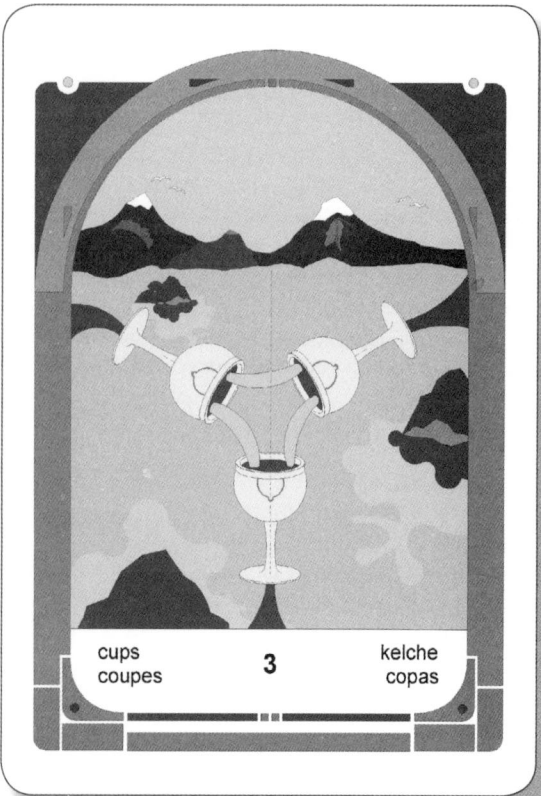

The 3 of Cups
Celebration, dancing, play

and partnerships that activate and magnetize our ideas. It helps us to bring others together, too. We like to be active and provide a place to invigorate your ideas.

⇒ IMAGINATION TOOLS
FROM THE THREE OF CUPS

- We gift you a tool to celebrate in your imagination.

- We gift you a tool to celebrate your imagination itself.

- We gift you a tool to celebrate with your imagination.

- We find that it has a tendency to burst out in smiles and songs when we dance!

The 4 of Cups

The 4 OF CUPS indicates to see the first signs of your desires' success as they begin to manifest. Good fortune and good luck are also indicated. A pause is present here which can be felt as stagnation on one hand if you are down. On the other hand, it is indicated that there is a still and powerful observation present. This flows from your thorough responsibility to what you do at this time. Step back to the 3 OF CUPS if you feel down. Get a little dance in your step for better observation here. Let your imagination feel your feet.

Focus with a sense of responsibility and enthusiasm is indicated. Feel your responsibility as natural and thorough. It is a natural part of the ways you brace your actions against the ground. Good fortune and good luck refresh the places where your labors start. Literally refresh the places where your labors start. Do this with simple enjoyment and a great deal of taste. Enjoy this place where the things you make have their first, complete mini-iteration.

Though stagnation is a possibility here, more so is an awareness to engage your core for your enjoyment! Enjoy what you make. You will nourish new ground for future things when you enjoy a taste of completion! There is a lot more to do. Pause here to feel what you make. Relish in it. Feel it. Keep it on track. Enjoy the taste of a success in a small completion here. Express it in your imagination, and write it down or sketch it.

The 4 of Cups
Life bursts forth, successes

Enter The 4 of Cups

Something new from your 4 OF PENTACLES experience bursts forth here to fulfill you and brighten and continue the celebration. Something may burst forth from the earth like a volcano! Something new may burst forth across your imagination and invigorate you, or blow something out to lighten your load. You have come to the place where the Earth of your imagination breathes and gives forth life. We place the four directions here. North, South, East, and West. They fill each cup to work with more facility and expand. Which one fills the cup from the volcano? Feel the new life that comes forth. Let it cool and incorporate to its natural place while you are here. It will be yours to take with you! We call our place the Image Nation. This is kind of like imagination with a twist. Image Nation. We are a place where the enjoyment of little successes cascades forward to support and enliven everything you do from here.

Here we love to see your desires start to manifest and bring you good fortune and good luck. Enjoy each little success as you explore here. The fruits of your labors will ripen later. They will ripen that much more if you begin to enjoy each and every little success along the way!

We are the place that puts together lots of 3 OF CUPS moments. This makes ideas vibrant and enjoyable. It also helps keep them healthy at every scale along the way as they grow. Remember the places between that connect. Remember your magical scale. We are all about them both here.

And, remember your tools! Sometimes you may feel things stagnate or slow or pause. But, with your tools, especially the ones that enhance your perspective, your awareness can lead to stronger feelings and show you how best to play with them. Fully enjoy the things you create. Enjoy every little success along the way.

We love thorough responsibility through and through. It really keeps us full as it moves us.

⇒ IMAGINATION TOOLS FROM THE FOUR OF CUPS

- We gift you a tool for new life to burst forth into your imagination!
- We gift you a tool to enjoy each and every little success along the way. You will ripen your ideas soon enough.

The 5 of Cups

The 5 OF CUPS indicates the experience of rough and turbulent times. You may feel perplexed. There is possible loss or loss that has already occurred. But, like the seagull, you can see something positive and bright in the tumultuous and choppy sea. This is hope that is in sight for the future. Simply scan your scene for a glimmer of magical hope. Cherish this hope like Pandora did when she found it. You can also discover it inside you. There is treasure in honest emotions.

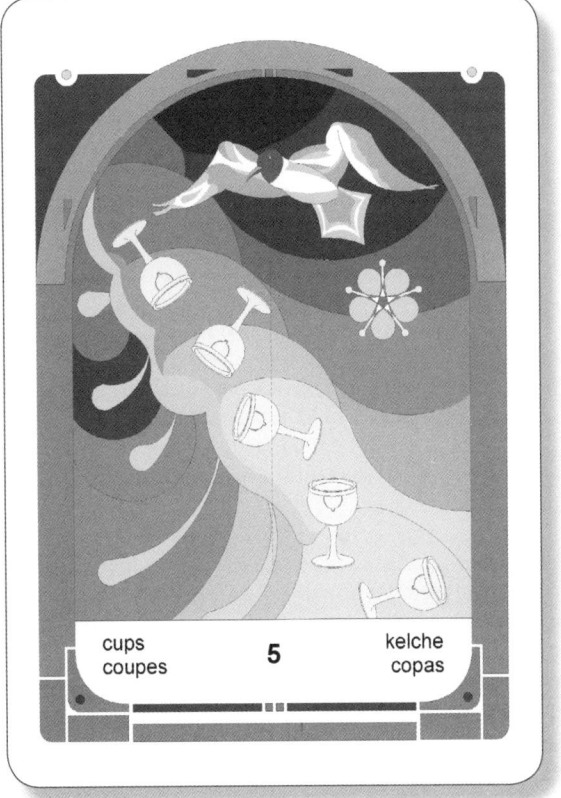

The 5 of Cups
Hidden treasure, emotional weather

Enter The 5 of Cups

No need to swim in these waters! That is not safe at all. Float-fly up here above the waves with your Magician wings outspread. Catch the currents and embrace the feel of your situation. Find a fresh perspective. Let the air currents flow under your wings and keep you refreshed. The currents' forces can nestle-push-flow-up under your wings and keep you in the air. This way, like the seagull, you scan around for the treasure in your situation. Float. It is a different kind of pause to learn for timing.

Scan around. Is it all so rough here? See any treasures besides the cups that you can so easily focus on? ☺ Yep. Right there behind the waves is a magical starfish. They know not to stand in front of stormy waves crashing. They can find a treasured place up here behind the waves until the storm has passed. Then, they settle back down to their place. What treasure do you feel in here with stormy waves?

As you weather this storm, find your treasure. Remember to feel it as you settle back in right at home with new things, like the magical starfish will after the storm.

We often experience rough and turbulent times in our 5 OF CUPS place. Recognize the hidden treasure of being perplexed. It may indicate that you are about to find something new. Like the magical starfish, it might hide in plain sight.

The seagull sees the treasure of a new discovery in its stormy sea. Like this seagull, our five cups tumble to discover hope for your future as you discover treasure in your emotions. Stick in there strongly, and keep your senses fresh as you move forward. Feel and find treasure even in a storm.

➣ *IMAGINATION TOOL* FROM THE FIVE OF CUPS

- We gift you a tool to see hidden treasures and find safe passage amidst even the most serious of emotional weather.

The 6 of Cups

The 6 OF CUPS indicates adjustments in thoughts and attitudes that create an ability to transcend difficulties. Equilibrium and balance of your emotions are also indicated. Connect to something in the past and explore your sentimental values. The things around you may give rise to new opportunities. View familiar things around you in a different way. Discuss your perspective with someone. Opportunities can stem from this exchange.

A connection or reconnection to something in your past – either to see an old acquaintance, pleasant memories of the past, perhaps even a message from someone you had lost contact with – is indicated. Familiar things seen in a different way often have the ability to refresh you.

Enter The 6 of Cups

Now you bring YOUR Cup to this place! See it right in front of you! The river here flows from the ACE OF CUPS' lake. She is fresh and flows through Mystereum. Wherever you see water in Mystereum you can be sure that she is there. Step in and feel free to fill your cup here. Adjust your ideas here with us. With your positive thoughts and a great attitude, your creativity can start to create a solid ability to transcend the difficulties in hard situations. We suggest that you not allow

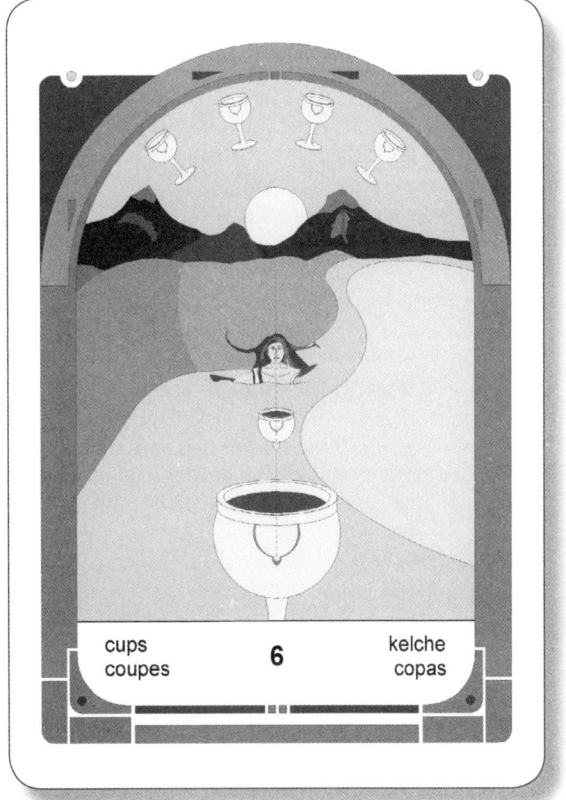

The 6 of Cups
Adjustments, balanced feelings, sharing

the hard situations to take root. Simply let them be. The ACE will come to help you flush 'em out soon enough.

This is the place to see balance in the ideas you hold in your cup. Wade on in. Share them and exchange them. You can move the cups around here as you switch focus with your 6 OF PENTACLES tools. Open your hands as ideas zip back up to the sky. Never half full or half empty, your cups can be a great place for the flower of an idea. Fill your cups with rockin' ideas that flow from your creativity.

➣ *IMAGINATION TOOL*
FROM THE SIX OF CUPS

- We gift you a tool of a balanced and refreshed place to explore and exchange portions of your ideas. Remember the weightlessness of your ideas and tools. You can fill and exchange a lot here with just the right amount of effort.

The 7 of Cups

The 7 OF CUPS indicates dreams or simply having your head in the clouds. Dreams are indicated to flourish at this time. Notice if your dreams encroach upon your situation at the expense of your actions. Mind to not get caught in your dream world at the expense of your actions and your reality. Take a big, deep breath. Visualize a great wind as you exhale. Increase your actions and clear the clouds and the chaff from your air with the newfound zeal of this great wind! It is a treasure to learn from the storm.

Dreams are wonderful, but not so much when by contrast their inspiration is lessened and they make disconnects in your actions. Balance and center and be clear. As with gardening, it is not recommended to cut things back too hard. In fact, do not cut things at all here. Simply increase your actions. Start with a big breath. All dreams and no action may be pie in the sky. It also may indicate that you are simply in a new place. Do not be afraid to act. Simply renew and think of that great wind. The clouds and chaff will begin to clear as the wheat of your dreams nourishes you with a newfound zeal.

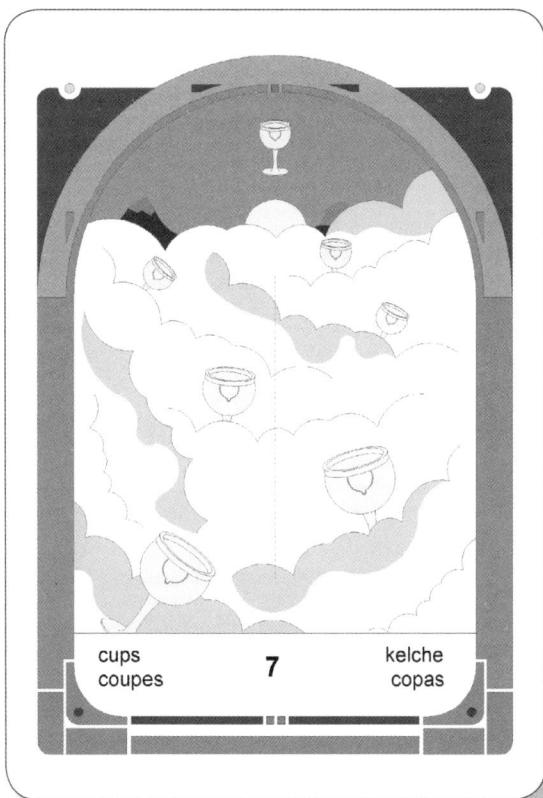

The 7 of Cups
Dreams, flourishing, ripening ideas

Enter The 7 of Cups

Remember your 7 OF PENTACLES tools now! Here in the place of the 7 OF CUPS, your ideas and dreams flourish. There are whole worlds in the clouds! Seven of them! Float-fly around here as you prepare your ideas to come forth. Be your own director. Your warm-up may be just about to NOT be a part of your performance. Blow out the head-in-the-clouds ideas that need to stay up here longer. They still have a ways to go. Weed and forget them for now. This is the place for your ideas to flourish. They are almost ready to perform.

Dreams are our first love here. They are your big ideas. They live in the clouds where your dreams flourish. Your head need not always be there, though. Check in on them to check their progress. Make sure they do not over-grow your actions. Notice each specific idea and dream. If it over-grows and encroaches at the expense of your actions, simply turn your focus and increase your actions with a big breath. Think of that great wind that clears clouds and chaff from your air. Some things simply look like ideas and dreams in the clouds. Get ready for your wonderful ideas to rain and fill your cups

⇒ *Imagination Tool*
From The Seven of Cups

- We gift you a tool of a great wind in your imagination to clear the ideas not ready to present yet. This way you can clearly see your star ideas. Not to worry. Some ideas that blow away along with the rest were not ready yet. They may return in a different way later.

The 8 of Cups

The 8 of Cups indicates a freeze-frame in your midst. You may feel this as listlessness or lack of purpose. You can also feel another proper pause. Move away from what no longer works to something new. Let in the laughable of your current situation. Travel to a new place, even if it is simply the park around the corner. Simply go a different way to get there. This may help to clear things up.

Feel free to pause your focus and deflate any troubled inertia as you move around in new surroundings! Notice the baby steps of new actions. They are like plant-noses poking up in a garden. Also, the 8 of Cups indicates to be neither patient nor anxious. Telling dahlias to hurry their growth may just be laughable to the dahlias. Sometimes it is best to let things clear up on their own time. Feel free to lower your focus to forget troubled movements. Forgetting is often for getting what your ideas miss here.

Enter The 8 of Cups

Begin to shift your pace here. At first you may feel that your head is still in the clouds. Breathe and watch. Breathe and feel. You can blow all the clouds away and focus more directly on your ideas. Your ideas have come together as a group to work together. Some will grow. Some will change

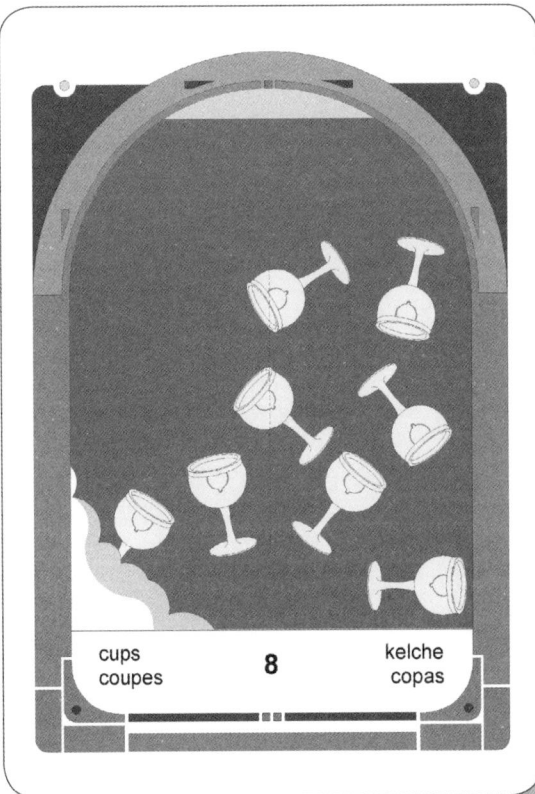

The 8 of Cups
Inner motions, settled, full

size to live in the details for you. Some will grow into a bigger picture. Pick and choose where each one lives in the whole. It is your call.

Listless feelings or a lack of purpose may come about if you do not shift to focus on the items in front of you. It is suggested not to move too fast here. There are arrangements and groups to be made to get your ideas ready to be put to work. Move away everything that no longer works. Arrange and orchestrate everything that does.

Remember how you cleared with the baby steps of a great wind of the 7 OF CUPS. Start a new action for each idea. Let in the laughable to your current situation. If something is funny, let it be. Laugh with it.

You may want to travel some with your new ideas to get some fresh perspectives as you drop the things that do not belong. Remember that forgetting is often for getting. Travel to a new place. See your current place differently. Replace what is missing with something new that works for you.

➵ *Imagination Tool*
From The Eight of Cups

- We gift you a tool of movement to discern things. Paint your whole scene with the ideas that move you.

The 9 of Cups

The 9 OF CUPS indicates happiness that starts within your mind. Flow emotions that are enthusiastic into the world. Inner happiness moves into the physical realm. A love of spirit is also indicated. Take a wonderful and respectful and invigorated note of blossoms and blooms as you celebrate the blossoms and blooms of your ideas!

Inner happiness moves into the physical realm to indicate to utilize your own, personalized HIEROPHANT abilities.

Enter The 9 of Cups

Welcome to the full wreath of our world! Our cups get their light from the sun in the middle. It is like a lightning bolt, but subtle in its strength. It endures like our personal sun. Our light lives in the clean pool the ACE OF CUPS gave us as a gift. Our cups are always ripe for you to pick and fill from the clean and sunny pool of your imagination. We grow down on our wreath like bells so that we are always clean and ready to receive your ideas as you pick us one by one. We will always grow back for you as you move forward. Our wreath is all about the manifestation of happiness that starts within the pool of your mind. Full emotions flow forth out into the world from here.

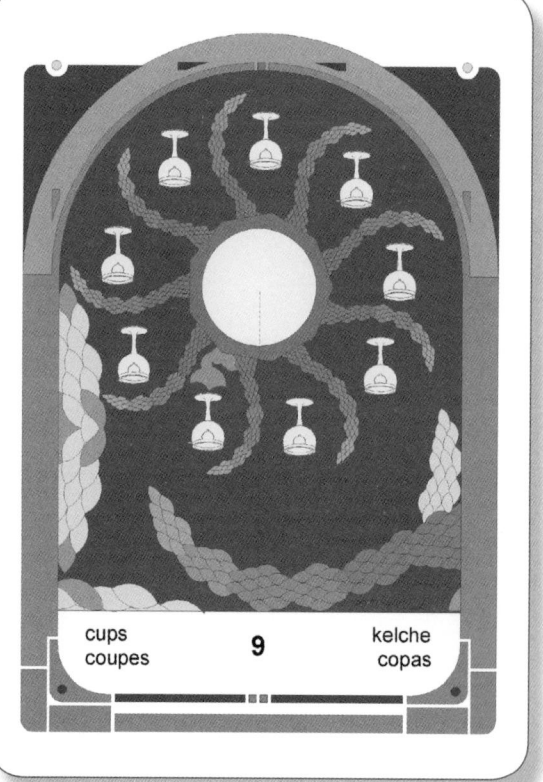

The 9 of Cups
Spirit, blossoms, blooms

We love that THE HIEROPHANT brought spirit down to earth. We have a down to earth spirit that fulfills us. We love that! We love wonderful respect for blossoms and blooms. Discover and nurture the blossoms and blooms in your idea solar system! Are there new ones?

⇒ IMAGINATION TOOL
FROM THE NINE OF CUPS

- We gift you the tool of a full wreath that always grows around a bright pool in your imagination. Tend to us and pick cups to embrace and hold your ideas. We grow cups for you here like bells. Let your ideas strike chords that resonate in them.

The 10 of Cups

The 10 of Cups indicates that you are in a great place to reflect with joy on your family and home. Great happiness, contentment, peace and love are also indicated. Count your blessings and work toward a goal that is centered on your home. Work together with your family or those close to you. Enjoy your ability to weather storms. Have fun watching from inside.

Work together to spruce up your home. Make it shine inside and out such that all benefit. If there is trouble in your family or home, joy may be realized if you work toward a goal together. The strength of a healthy family weathers any storm. The strength of a healthy family shines inside and out such that all benefit. Express your joy with a surprise hidden in plain sight, a token sent in an altogether different way. Get creative. Odds are you have a flow that is priceless right now. Share it.

If you are far from family, treat the family of your ideas and experiences with the same powerful and grand love you would for someone special that you love. Family is forever as you are forever in it. As many a wise 14-year-old-sage has said, "We are all immortal until we die." Step up to explore the humor and wisdom in that. Love your experiences.

Enter The 10 of Cups

We love the joy we feel when we reflect on family and home. Great happiness, contentment, peace, and love shine right in.

We love to count our blessings and fulfill ourselves as we work toward a goal together.

We love that the strength of a healthy family shines inside and out such that all benefit. We love that a healthy family of people and ideas can weather any storm and grow stronger.

⇒ *IMAGINATION TOOL*
FROM THE TEN OF CUPS

- We gift you the tool to feel the strength that shines inside and out when everything you love works together!

The 10 of Cups
Reflection, sharing, home

The Page of Cups

The PAGE OF CUPS indicates to care for someone and playful and fun thoughts of loved ones. Musical and artistic talents are also indicated as the Page flows new things in. The strength of an enthusiastic character that is passionate and follows dreams may be present.

Watch big cats slowly sweep their cubs off their feet. This play may teach the cubs how to catch dinner in the future.

Watch for new emotions that fulfill you!

Enter The Page of Cups

I AM The PAGE OF CUPS.

I love that you care for someone and that your ideas and thoughts are playful and fun.

I love for you to have a love for your ideas.

I love musical and artistic talent.

I love being loved, and love the strength of the energetic characters that fill you up.

The Page of Cups
New love, self-discovery, swimming

I love it when you follow your dreams with bright passion. It excites me when you bring them into Your Royal Court for all of Mystereum to herald!

☞ *Imagination Tool*
From The Page of Cups

- I gift you a tool to bring forth your discoveries as you work with The Hanged Man, The Empress, The Emperor, and The Ace of Cups. Be afloat in clarity as your journey refreshes you. May you frolic and swim in your Royal Court!

The Knight of Cups

The Knight of Cups indicates that things have taken on an emotional and intuitive way. Trust the strength of your feelings. Emotion and intuition are valiant! They lead the way to your destination! Feel in to this! Incorporate your ideas across the board.

The Knight of Cups world is a place where the new emotions brought in by the Page of Cups are incorporated. This is a place to move your ideas around by using them, move them around by putting them into action. Brand new feelings naturally begin to become new core feelings here. Notice how things are placed and fulfilled in your world. Notice how you begin to place things more naturally.

You may have new feelings about your sense of your life in general. These new feelings very naturally and quickly may begin to belong as if they have always been with you. Feel a natural sense of ease with these newfound treasures as you put them to use with your ideas. Do you have new feelings, even subtle sprouts of them, that *feel* very natural and go wonderfully well with your ideas? The Knight of Cups will help you to put them into action as the treasures that they are. You may be opening up some more of the treasures of your inner inheritances.

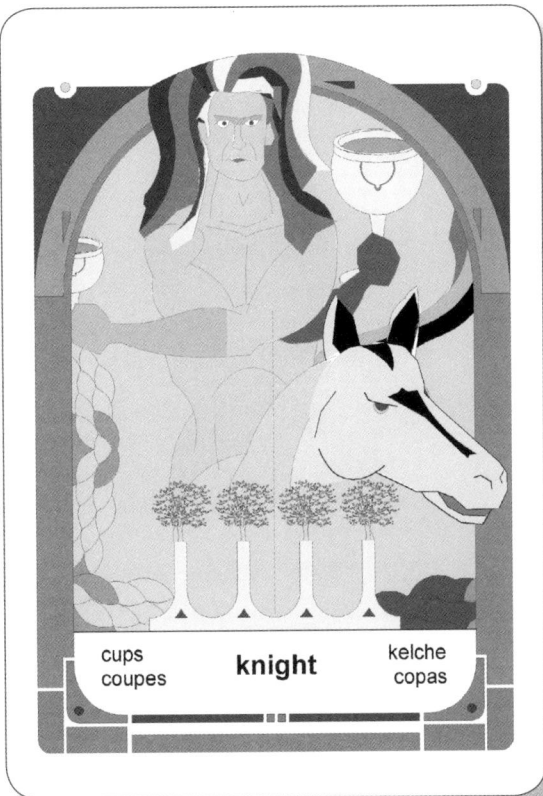

The Knight of Cups
Valiant feelings, honest expressions

Enter The Knight of Cups

I AM The Knight of Cups.

I love that things have taken on an emotional and intuitive way.

I love the honesty and strength inherent in situations where you incorporate communication from your core.

I love when emotions and intuitions lead the way on your journey.

⇒ *Imagination Tool*
From The Knight of Cups

- I gift you a tool to trust the depth and strength of your emotions. May there be a Chariot to connect the depths of your inner world to your sky as you ride forth and replenish Your Royal Court. Fulfill Your Royal Court with the new energies you incorporate.

The Queen of Cups

The QUEEN OF CUPS indicates harmony in your emotional and intuitive realms. Rely on inner guidance and an inner perspective that is thick and flows with richness. Your perspective is well suited to respond to external influences at this time. Your natural leadership abilities can take charge in matters of your inner life. Draw upon the wisdom of the ages that is natural to you. Imagination. Creativity. Love. Support. Feel these with your emotions.

This is a time when your strong imagination may sense hidden depths that are not readily apparent! Express your emotions confidently at this time.

Odds are you are also very impressionable at this time. In the positive this indicates a strong feeling-sense. It indicates an ability to be influenced to your benefit. As still waters run deep, there are hidden depths not readily apparent.

The QUEEN OF CUPS indicates a natural and charismatic leader with an ability to express emotions confidently and clearly.

The Queen of Cups
Discerning clearly, hidden depths seen

Enter The Queen of Cups

I AM the QUEEN OF CUPS.

I am in harmony with my emotional and intuitive realms.

I wholeheartedly rely on my inner guidance so that my inner perspective and flow are thick and rich.

I love when you take charge in matters of your inner life where your emotions draw upon the wisdom of the ages.

Your imagination and creativity support a strong and natural feeling-sense that will lead you to hidden depths that are not always readily apparent.

➢ *IMAGINATION TOOL* FROM THE QUEEN OF CUPS

- I gift you the tool of the wisdom of the ages whether you have learned them or not. I feel that the wisdom of the ages is already natural and present in your emotions. May you always act in accord with the wisdom you feel is best for YOUR ROYAL COURT.

The King of Cups

The KING OF CUPS indicates a protective figure of abundance that protects by simply being supportive. He indicates for you to feel prosperity inside and out. Guidance is not provided here. This KING finds inspiration in conversation. Feel the joyousness as groups shine in conversation!

Rather than a guide that shows the path, this KING indicates to be supportive and protective. Be a friend and companion on the track of life. Your abilities to inspire in simple conversation shine as those around you sip from the cup of your abundant energy. This is a grand time to have a get-together and flow wonderfully with those close to you!

Be it small or be it big, flow with those you care about.

Enter The King of Cups

I AM the KING OF CUPS.

I am a protective figure of abundance.

I support and protect rather than guide.

I shine in the joyousness of groups.

I have wonderful get-togethers where peoples' abilities shine in conversation.

May you flow wonderfully with those you care about.

➣ *Imagination Tool* From The King of Cups

- I gift you the full love and attention of everything and everyone in Your Royal Court to make a life that is magnetic and draws wonderful things into your kingdom over the years and beyond.

This is what I wish for you.

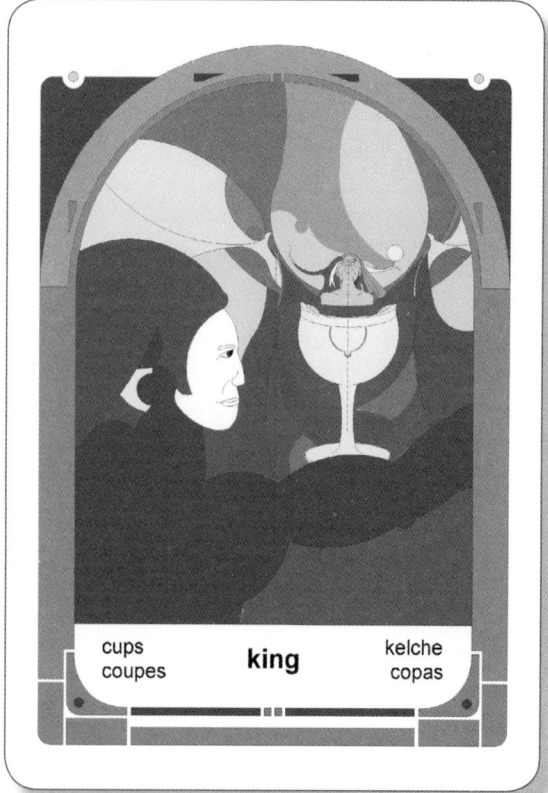

The King of Cups
Supportive, prosperity, conversation

Notes

PART FOUR

Energizing Imagination

The Fool's Journey Through Wands

The Ace of Wands

The ACE OF WANDS indicates new life born that begins to make place. A sacred staff is set here by THE HERMIT to locate a place and bless its future structure. A sage ritual often follows. It is also indicated to re-make the place where you work. Clear the clutter and arrange things to provide a strong place for new energies to find a home. Celebrate energy flow as you increase its power!

Creativity is indicated in the act of placement. Courage is indicated in the placement itself. This brings enthusiasm to the energy of places being made.

Enter The Ace of Wands

WHOOSH! VROOM! WOW, You sure just turned THAT page! What a SMILE! WOW! Everything here is NEW NEW NEW! That page may get turned millions of times, and I simply LOVE IT every single time! WHOOSH!

When you turned that page it cleaned off EVERYTHING about it. You must have already met my sis, The ACE OF CUPS! Cool Kewel! Great girl she is! She was born to fill things cleanly. I was born to energize new places! I have a fire of pure energy, and energize things to magnetize fresh new energies to find their place. She will fill your eyes, and I will light them up for you. All you have to do to make us

The Ace of Wands
New life, place-making, enthusiasm

work is have an ear to ear smile! When you laugh, we work together for you! Pretty simple, huh?

I just dig that page turning thing! One day I may meet whoever made that page turning thing up. Thinkin' it is way back in wand history before me. No matter if I do not meet them, though. I will always know I still have one more historical friend way back there, and another at the turn of a page. I like to turn pages. Fanning them spreads their energy!

I love new life. I taught priests and master builders of old how to set their sacred staff to locate the place of a building or a meeting space. They used the sacred staff called an omphallos to set and make place. I feel that place-making is important. I love to locate a building. I love to locate a space. I get excited when I locate a place to play! My favorite thing is to make a place for a set of ideas!

A place. Hmmm. What is that? You *see* I do not direct my energies just anywhere. It may look all fast and instantaneous like lightning when I act, but everything comes before that instant. You have already met a lot of my teachers here in Mystereum. They are really more like friends who teach me a great deal. I do not think they know they teach me. No matter. I act with play after a lot of planning. A lot of forgetting goes in to my aim to feel JUST the right place to place things.

I love the creativity in the act of placement and the courage of the placement itself. The enthusiastic energy in newly made places is my favorite!

Imagination Tool
From The Ace of Wands

- I gift you the ability to direct your energies so that you can place them exactly where you feel best. You will meet up later with a Queen who will tell you about levels of force while doing this. But, for now, simply feel your energies, and begin to understand about their placements within you. It will make it more fun as you go along to turn them up and down and find out for yourself what resonates with each and every situation's energy.

The 2 of Wands

The 2 OF WANDS indicates a warning of potential disaster by overload and imbalance. Settle back to your ACE. Look for your natural path. Do not become overwhelmed and perceive many little things as one big thing. Be aware if you daydream. See any fixations that hold your focus too tightly as mirages. You direct your focus not the other way around.

Listen. Wait. Feel. Be on the move to pull you through this time where you may feel barraged. There is a lot going on here.

Do not blindly move when you are here. Look for your natural path. Again, do not perceive many little things as one big thing. Cannot say that enough. There is often one thing reflected through everything to appear as many things. There is magic in the mirror. Also, do not let it fool you. Preconceptions seen here may be fixations to drop. Daydream a little while you listen. Wait. Be on the move like THE HERMIT, aware of his cycles and reiterations. Incorporate the new iterations. Feel through any reflections that are delusions or mirages. Feel through them. Feel past them. Use your great wind as you keep on the move.

The 2 of Wands
Directed focus, seeing past tricksters

Enter The 2 of Wands

It is okay. Come on in! Our sky is different than any other sky in Mystereum. THE HERMIT cracked open night and day here for us to work with together like a puzzle. Do not mind all the moons on the right. There is still only one moon here. Be careful of that guy, though. He thinks there are too many moons. The mirror fools him. He still has not seen through his own mirage. Understand when you play with pretend.

I would like to show you about how to keep your wits and your head about you even when you are completely perplexed. We find that this can happen when you use a different perspective. We suggest your perspective! Our sky simply looks confusing with so many moons. Our 2 OF WAND's sky is a lesson in itself: Do not perceive many little things as one big thing. Think and feel the many perspectives of only one moon here! Understand that when you feel perplexed, it may be that you do not see with your own perspective.

We are here for your imaginative path. Our biggest strength is to not be perplexed by perception. An initial feeling often sticks, but our eyes and our thoughts have to catch up. We are here to show you that when you feel overwhelmed it often means to change the scale of your focus. Get bigger. Get smaller. Flex your temples as you direct your focus.

There is a difference between a daydream and the distraction of hope in vain. We would rather not perceive preconceptions or fixations. They make big ole blind spots with expectations. Rather, we love to feel what IS! We love to listen and wait. We do not put ourselves on hold. We flex our temples!

We love being on the move like our friend and mentor THE HERMIT. That is fun, too. We hang out with THE CHARIOT just as much. Keep that smile while you flex those temples! It is the order of the day here! There is place to make here! It is serious business at this stage. Gotta start in the right place. Gotta feel it first and then bring the lightning of the omphallos to earth!

Surprised? We turn on a dime here. It is just fine to track back to where we met and follow along again as you get your pace just right here. We do not pull any punches here. We know there is a lot going on. Do not fear what you feel. Feel it. Let it inform you to listen. Breathe and feel to inform your wait. Know what you feel. Make sure you feel settled as you place things. Where you place things first is of the utmost importance here.

⇒ *IMAGINATION TOOL*
FROM THE TWO OF WANDS

- We gift you the tool to shift your focus and redirect your scale on the fly if you feel perplexed. We gift you this to see and feel what IS as you establish places for your ideas!

The 3 of Wands

The 3 OF WANDS indicates a new enthusiasm for your ideas. Find places for them. Plan your work or career partnerships to make a great way for success. Possible travel is indicated as you look for the best places for these energies. Enjoy a grand view from newly created places or places you have traveled!

With your enthusiasm, also look at and plan to drive your further success. Now is a grand time for partnerships in your work and play. Travel or communications with distant places is indicated. You have a good perspective with the new enthusiasm you have.

Enter The 3 of Wands

COOL! New energy! Come on IN! What's your name?! We are at a pretty small scale here! We full-on DIG IT! See our wands as they fly across from left to right? They always cross from left to right. New energies come in here on the left, pass through to invigorate us, and continue on their journey. Quite the cycle here! They give just enough to keep us fresh as they move. They do not deplete anything! The 6 OF PENTACLES likes it here, too. Anything new just come to you? May we ask what? ☺ Please write it down.

The 3 of Wands
New energies, enthusiasm, travel

We love a world where success is present and kept fresh. This is a place where good things succeed and a good pace of motion is part of the plan. We plan for the long term. It is a grand time for partnerships in your work or career. You may even travel across the world. Simply make a trip across the yard or a park that changes your scene! There are new energies everywhere you let them in to cycle across for you. We suggest that you bring good energies in to brighten you.

We love a good view from places just created. It is like when cookies come out of the oven to us. That's the BEST!

⇒ *IMAGINATION TOOL* FROM THE THREE OF WANDS

- We gift you the tool of fresh, new, and positive energies that always come into your imagination from unseen sources to keep you fresh. Feel them!

The 4 of Wands

The 4 OF WANDS indicates the joy as people and ideas come together for a purpose, and the growth and fulfillment that results. A surprise or thrill out of the blue is also indicated. You may meet someone unexpectedly. Plan celebrations.

Enjoy the freedom you may feel when you build something with someone who enhances your energies. Plan to celebrate and reap abundance together! Let any sorrow or dissatisfaction simply disappear into the ground

Enter The 4 of Wands

Surprise! Look at how well-placed and solid your energies are! New things begin to come in all the time. Keep them healthy! We suggest that you make some subtle adjustments. You may see the proper order of things in an altogether different way! This is the place where we arrange energies and ideas with joy! This is our purpose. It makes for growth and happiness!

A surprise or thrill that comes out of the blue is common here. So, we plan celebrations all the time with extra seats. We express our freedom and build things together. Abundance is natural and is reaped with joy.

The 4 of Wands
Joy, surprises, thrills out of the blue

⇝ *Imagination Tool*
From The Four of Wands

- We gift you the tool to arrange energy in your imagination with joy. Red is great! But, heavy is better. Have fun and place your ideas just so. Give them the weight and life they deserve!

The 5 of Wands

The 5 OF WANDS indicates stiff competition that is not necessarily fair. A challenge with no clear winner implied is also indicated. Enterprise and glory are present. Rev up and warm up your engine to prepare for obstacles you perceive ahead. Shift and corner with a new perspective that the competition does not have!

Notice how each wand has a separate identity simply by their placement. Your challenge may have an unclear outcome. Remember that your enterprise and glory rule your wands here. This may be like when you rev the engine and the clutch is in. Strong competition often indicates obstacles. Do not stop your forward movement. Add your new perspective to the mix. Add a perspective that the competition does not have.

Feel the wonders of the objects and systems outside of you. Feel your actions in place that originate from the places inside you.

Enter The 5 of Wands

Come join our game of catch as catch can! You see, when you do not take these things personally, you will have wonderful wits about you. You may even be funny as you prevail! We suggest you keep everything simple

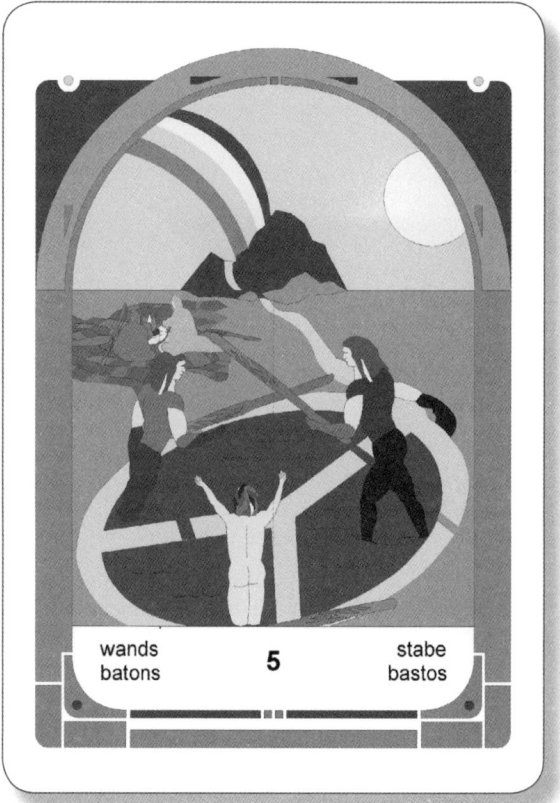

The 5 of Wands
Stiff competition, challenges, new perspective

here. Too much energy is already here to add a bunch more. Do not make things more cloudy. Be like the child who has dropped his wand here. He sees a rainbow in the mix that no-one else has seen.

Harness these energies! The others are simply too excited to have seen through their blinds spots to the rainbow you can see. Ever been in a situation when the odds felt too noisy? Can you remember something you felt that helped align the situation? Or, maybe you felt something that would be useful to align powerful and excited energies in your future?

Our QUEEN OF WANDS taught us to see through our blind spots. Our SUN taught us that no matter how cloudy our day he is still there to shine for us. There is stiff competition here that does not seem fair at first. Love your enterprise and your glory. First feel and then see the positive direction of your challenge. No clear winner is implied. Yet, you are here.

Steer your eyes to the rainbow here. Do not lose sight of all the activity as you do. Include the rainbow. Notice that there are two people sitting over there on the left. Are they tired? Talking? Waiting to talk to you? No matter. Express your energies with a smile. That may make it 3 on 2. Then, maybe 5 that act together! One for each color of the rainbow can come together to the mountain.

This place is about when you act in the moment! THE CHARIOT taught us that. He taught us balance in our motion even when everything feels to be about to shake apart. He taught us to tune our situation and exceed! Strategy in action at speed is wonderfully active here.

We suggest a physical meditation of the flow of your imagination here. Direct your creative action at speed as you work all these energies into harmony.

➛ IMAGINATION TOOLS
FROM THE FIVE OF WANDS

- We gift you the tool to discover crucial pieces that bring a situation together. These are pieces that can be found in your imagination and seen around you. We gift you this tool so you can better enhance your ability to express the crucial pieces of any situation.

The 6 of Wands

The 6 OF WANDS indicates receiving victory and glory. Overcoming obstacles is indicated through teamwork as you keep your channels clear and tuned in this glorious time! New energies are coming in as if cascading into your spirit from above. Feel the wash of these new flows like soft tides and waves of energy from above as they arrive for you.

These new energies may actually serve to lighten your load later. They may wash away old things, and as well they may make you stronger to play with the ideas you have with a greater ease. This is a time for more actions than words as you feel the interchange between the energies of your ideas. Put your ideas together in creative ways to see how they begin working on their own so you can see them and have them inform you more of their natural energies. Simply enjoy them; almost as a spectator you feel the new grooves of these natural idea energies.

Enter The 6 of Wands

Bask in victory and glory here! Simply raise your head and hands up and feel the energy that comes in for you! We would like to invite you to explore your energy here a while. There is a lot for you to receive which we feel will lighten

The 6 of Wands
Victory, glory, overcoming obstacles

your load later. Feel the wonderful and strong energy that fits just right with you.

Team up your ideas and energy. Add some teammates to overcome obstacles. You can divide and conquer that way. We say very few words. We simply feel the energy and the energy exchanges made here. Your smile will do quite nicely when you feel the right things that arrive right in front of you.

➣ IMAGINATION TOOL
FROM THE SIX OF WANDS

- We gift you the tool to feel the victory and glory you receive from your ideas!

The 7 of Wands

The 7 OF WANDS indicates to take affirmative and decisive action even though you may feel outnumbered or swamped by adversity. The glow of success here is indicated to be that much brighter when you succeed.

Feeling outnumbered or swamped by adversity may indicate a false summit! False summits are just that. Summits, "mountaintops" that are false. There is still a long way to go. Strategize and see things in a different way.

The 7 OF WANDS indicates to go in headlong and take affirmative and decisive action. Success is indicated even when you feel outnumbered or swamped by adversity. With the right aim you can zip right through or join up with the energies in place.

Enter The 7 of Wands

Woo Hoo, YAH! You are doing it! Go for it! You see the way! Remember those birds you see who fly full speed into the tree to instantly land right on their target softly! How do they do that? Remember THE CHARIOT in that moment while visualizing that bird. Sync up and link yourself to the other side of your aim. Put all that together and you can act deliberately!

The 7 of Wands
Decisive action, strategies, taking charge

Go in headlong? Take affirmative and decisive action? Yes. This is a time when it is indicated you can succeed by doing so.

Do you feel out-numbered or swamped by adversity? Are you really? Maybe you can find a fresh perspective that the situation needs. Sometimes being outnumbered or swamped by adversity can simply be a false summit kind of feeling. You may feel other peoples' fears. Be thoughtful and mindful of yours and others' feelings. But, once you get your bearings and feel what you personally feel, take action!

There's an old Chinese proverb that goes:

~ It is the right thing to do to respect the right of way. Also, those who say it cannot be done should get out of the way of the person doing it.

This is what happens most in our part of Mystereum!

⇒ *Imagination Tool*
From The Seven of Wands

- We gift you a tool to fully feel your ideas in action as you take charge and make them real! Be deliberate.

The 8 of Wands

The 8 OF WANDS indicates a positive change of mind with your health, your new ideas, and your goals. Revisit projects and ideas that you have in the works. Letters of love or thanks, communications, or a journey by air travel are also indicated. Feel the way your mind travels when you are in open spaces or a garden. You may love field sports. With an active interest focus on the things that are "up in the air" in a positive way for you!

Gardening. Field sports. The indication is that things are "up in the air" in a positive way. This is more of an active interest than a wait. There is a powerful witness when you watch with interest and activity. Participate as you see how things turn out.

Enter The 8 of Wands

Enjoy the decisive actions you just made in our 7! Let the results settle. Here is the place where your energies are like moonbeams. Moonbeams are up in the air in a positive way! We deal with positive changes of mind with our health, our new ideas, our goals, our projects in the works, our letters of love all with our energetic communication. We like to be close to these energies. We love to take journeys by air travel, with love, or simply with a love of open spaces.

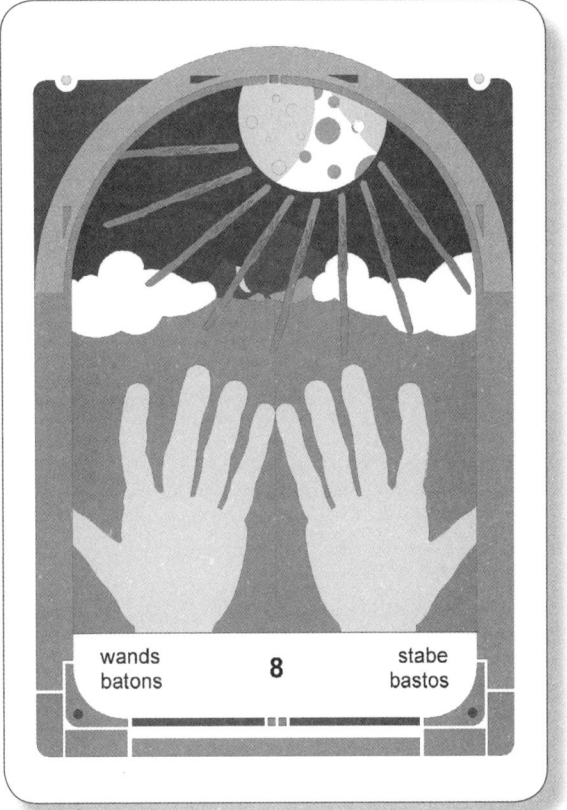

The 8 of Wands
Positively up in the air, field sports

Gardening, tennis, volleyball, and field sports are an active interest for us. They are things that we play that have a quality of "something positive is up in the air." We also love that our 8 is not only a pair of 4s and your first manifestations. The 8 is also an upright infinity like its picture has been taken as it is flying through the air. Mind this place as a park on the mountain. Rather than a false summit, play here for a while until you are ready to move your dynamic ideas up the mountain of your process further!

⇒ *IMAGINATION TOOLS* FROM THE EIGHT OF WANDS

- We gift you the tool of a high level place to play when you are waiting! Enjoy being up in the air from time to time. Do not wait and be bored. Make it fun. No time or problems are wasted here. Play with an active mind.
- We gift you the thought that an active mind is immune to boredom. How cool is THAT?!

The 9 of Wands

The 9 OF WANDS indicates that your preparation is complete. You have a pause of commencement with your ideas. Sit back and take a deep breath. Look into the distance with a smile. Feel a wonderful contentedness in the great activity here. This is an auspicious time to have a great get-together! Or, nail that important presentation! It is indicated that you feel ready. Take one big breath before the first guests arrive or before you start your presentation. Take one big breath and smile! Deliver with enthusiasm and let your celebration begin! Hang back for one more second and breathe deep. Look into your distance and smile. A wonderful feeling of contentment may fill you.

Ding dong! Let the celebration begin! Start your presentation!

Enter The 9 of Wands

☺ Look at how far you have come! Look at how much you have done! We are one complete piece that you can use over and over to energize bigger and bigger things. We are not about those bigger things, though. We are the place where your energies come to a point of completeness. We are a place where your situations are built with consistency as you build with your strengths. We have set up some

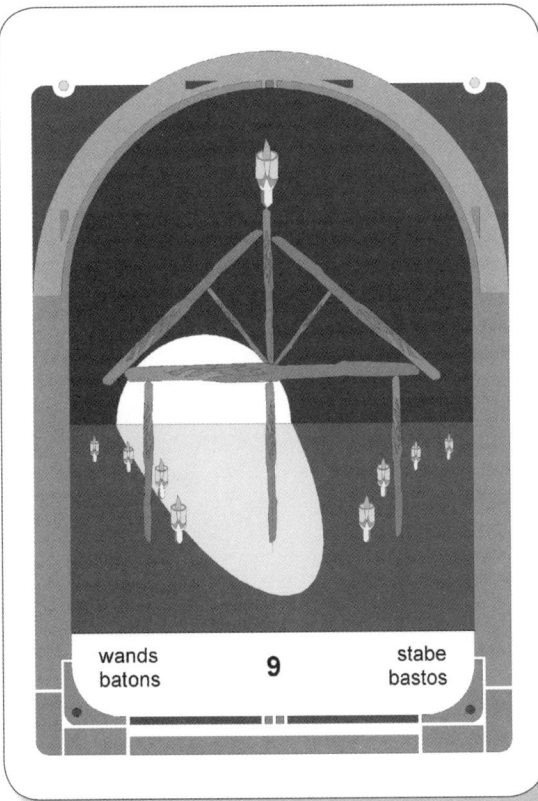

The 9 of Wands
Preparation complete, pause, commencement

lanterns for you. With your own decorations, you can plan a fun get-together here in the moonlight! We are ready for the guests to arrive. Your preparation is complete here. Now is the time to see your ideas in action.

We love that the preparation is complete. We love the pause of commencement before the first guests arrive. Like your guests, we love to see all that you have done for us. We love that moment right before you start your great presentation! Hang back and take a big breath before you proceed further here. Look into the distance and smile across all that you have put together. We love the wonderful feeling of being content that fills your air right in front of you.

Ding dong. There is the doorbell! Let the celebration begin!

⇒ IMAGINATION TOOL
FROM THE NINE OF WANDS

- We gift you the tool to notice and breathe in that wonderfully brief moment of peace and tranquility right before your festivities start up! Remember this time. You can use it over and over as you complete your work and provide your perspective to mark the moment!

The 10 of Wands

The 10 OF WANDS indicates the balance and courage you show. There is an agility and a strong balance of all you carry indicated. Here you tow everything with the grace of your own body. Each twilight sky prefigures the night just as dawn loves the promise of the coming day. Love wonderful new challenges as the twilight and dawn love the night and the day!

There is courage to own what you carry and invigorate it. Also, let it invigorate you. Blind faith to fulfill your purpose will express the balance like juggling. Transformation is set in motion by passion and direction in your principles. Agility with wonderfully strong balance indicates that you may juggle your ideas so well and naturally that they appear to orbit in a solar system. Your idea solar system?

Enter The 10 of Wands

I love the energetic balance that you have shown in your courage along your journey in Mystereum! I love the energy of your agility. I love your strong balance with all you carry! I love that you are able to balance your energies so well that you learn how to tow everything with the simple grace of your own body!

The 10 of Wands
Balanced courage, agility, grace

I love the energy of each twilight sky that introduces you to the night. I love the energy of the dawn sky as it awakens the promise of the day. I love the energy of each day to bring wonderful new challenges. I love the energy of each night to bring you wonderful dreams!

⇒ *IMAGINATION TOOL*
FROM THE TEN OF WANDS

- I gift you the tool of wonderful balance throughout your idea solar system. May you tune and tailor all that is there. May you tow your ideas with the grace of your own *mindbodybeautiful* as you explore, create, and make their orbits.

The Page of Wands

The PAGE OF WANDS indicates a powerful rush of excitement that offers an adventure or a risk. News and information that will assist you on your path with a sense of adventure are also indicated. This may be by a change in attitude about your environment as a whole. Notice if your environment has already changed. With industrious efforts, it is indicated that you can be fluid and reinforce your adventure as new energies enter for your benefit. Begin to bring them in well. Move with enthusiasm full of exuberance and creativity!

The Page of Wands is a young charioteer here full of youthful exuberance, creativity, and character. Remember this powerful shift: Risk transforms into scope once you have poured forth your efforts. There is consequently no longer risk. There is a scope of work to be done. It is composed of your priorities. Your direction is very present in the things around you. It is indicated is to move with strength and modesty. This does not preclude bold moves. It simply indicates that broad brush strokes are inappropriate.

Take care with the formwork of your actions. Formwork is to the foundation as the pond turning over is to the pond. It holds a curing process to refresh order. Remember that the pond remembers its turning over only in its continued fertility. Feel that as you are fluid and build foundations for the most adventurous paths of your dreams. Dig deep.

The Page of Wands
Rush of excitement, adventure, risk

Enter The Page of Wands

I AM The Page of Wands.

I love the powerful rush of excitement offered by an adventure or risk. I love the births of ideas as they awaken in the energies of my emotions.

I love to continue on paths of adventure where there is a necessity of a change in attitudes about the environment as a whole. This refreshes me.

I love industrious and disciplined efforts that release your imagination to be fluid and build a substantial base for yourself.

I love being a young charioteer. I love being a messenger full of exuberance and creativity!

⇒ *Imagination Tool* From The Page of Wands

- I gift you a tool to birth your discoveries using The Moon, The Star, The Sun, The Chariot, Strength, Judgment, and the 10 of Wands. May you bring new energies from deep and dark places into the celestial light of Your Royal Court! May your magical renewal awake!

The Knight of Wands

The KNIGHT OF WANDS indicates a pause with too great of an emphasis on spiritual matters and un-reflected actions. Be mindful of new and unfamiliar actions and feelings. Visualize the house that cracks open here not as hard to mend damage. See this house that cracks open as an awakening!

It is also indicated that you may feel introspection and flux. Transition and healing are very present. Feel renewal as you awaken to more spirit. Actively grow from your spiritual core! Your inner house may have cracked open simply to awaken and grow further. Respect the delicate nature of the new things that come into your mix. Incorporate them with careful attention.

Your house is in some form of flux, transition, healing, renewal, or awakening. Be concrete. Be very observant. Keep your balance across the board. Develop things in an active environment.

Enter The Knight of Wands

I AM The KNIGHT OF WANDS. If I pause with too great an emphasis on spiritual matters and un-reflected actions, it is often because I feel new and unfamiliar feelings.

The Knight of Wands
Unfamiliar actions, feelings, awakening

I love to awaken in this pause where my internal house crack-hatches again. I love that this is not hard to mend damage. I love that this is an AWAKENING!

I love it when you grow from your spiritual core and the renewal it brings to Your Royal Court.

➤ IMAGINATION TOOL
FROM THE KNIGHT OF WANDS

- I gift you a tool to birth and incorporate your discoveries using THE HIEROPHANT, STRENGTH, JUDGMENT, THE STAR and the 10 OF WANDS.

Spiritually strengthened through and through may you awaken into the newly balanced You. Appear and come forth from deep and dark places and bring your celestial light to YOUR ROYAL COURT!

The Queen of Wands

The QUEEN OF WANDS indicates a great power to attract your wants. There is an abundance of mind and body with a fire of life. Clear and magical energetic vision is also indicated. Dreams are the heartbeat of all of her actions. You may feel her love of nature and home. You may benefit with practicality in regards to money. Feel the life-acumen of her natural leadership.

With strong and intense and enjoyable balances of business and pleasure infuse life into every step! Emotional content in action makes a complete scenario. Infuse life into every step and use important mundane details to your benefit.

Kindness and generosity are indicated. With the QUEEN OF WANDS you are no sleeping lion. You are awake and present and strong to the degree that there is nothing to prove. Nothing may feel new. Feel the freshness of originality throughout everything. Your sense of smell may increase.

Visualize the life of a tiger as you tow your life with the weight of your own body. Your grace and strength and passion fuel your dreams. They are the heartbeat of all you do. Feel the magic of your dreams breathe life into your actions.

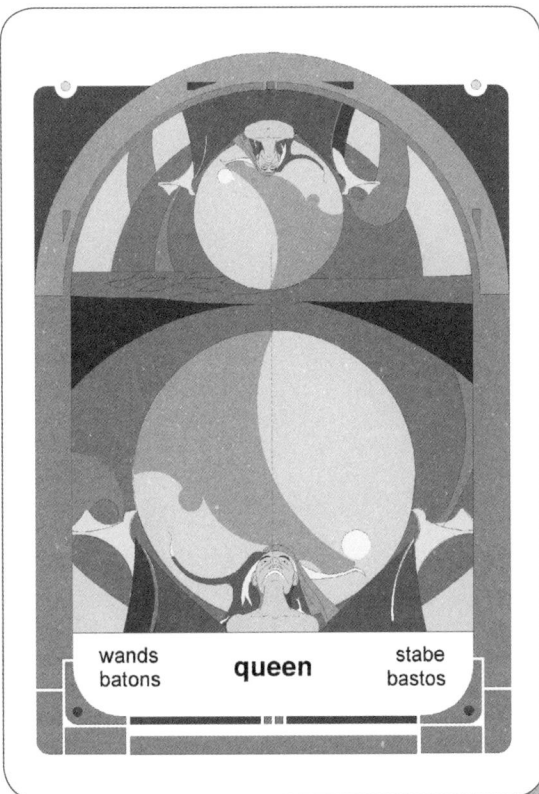

The Queen of Wands
Attracting wants, fire of life, life-acumen

Enter The Queen of Wands

I AM the QUEEN OF WANDS.

Your vision is blessed and sacred and trusted.

I love my great power to attract my wants with the abundance I feel in my mind and body. My dreams are the heartbeat of all my actions. My dreams are the fire of my life.

I love nature and home together.

My practicality with money comes from my life-acumen. I am strong with exquisite balances of business and pleasure.

I love complete scenarios. My emotional content clarifies my vision and breathes life into each step.

⇒ *IMAGINATION TOOL*
FROM THE QUEEN OF WANDS

- I gift you the tool that your vision is blessed and sacred and magical.

The King of Wands

The KING OF WANDS indicates charismatic leadership within you that is natural. Your natural flow influences things. Now is the time to get done what needs to be done, and this king loves that it will get done! Enjoy as you get things done! Once complete, it is indicated that everyone will be pleased with the results.

Enter The King of Wands

I AM the KING OF WANDS.

Charismatic leadership is within you and flows from you.

Your flow has great influence. Feel that.

I love that now is often the best time to get done what needs to be done. I love that what needs to get done will get done!

I love that once complete, everyone will be enthusiastic about the results.

The King of Wands
Complete energies, acting in the moment

➤ *Imagination Tool*
From The King of Wands

- I gift you complete energies to be able to act in the moment as you build vibrant life throughout your kingdom and Your Royal Court.

These are the things I wish for you.

Notes

Part Five

Communicative Imagination | The Fool's Journey Through Swords

The Ace of Swords

The ACE OF SWORDS indicates to cut through complex ideas and make things clear. This is done when you stick to the point. It is indicated to stand up for yourself even when there is no certainty of your placement. Meditate options before you take the next logical step. This is the place to identify and understand causes. Feel them directly.

Utilize discretion as you trust your inner, personal convictions. Cut through the bull as you stick to the point. Be mindful of impersonal, indifferent, or even bossy expressions. Do not let down your guard. Visualize your guard and armor simply as the state of your health. Keep your wits about you and your health strong. Keep your thoughts on point. The ACE OF SWORDS presents an opportunity to cut through confusion and shed light on situations that cause difficulty.

Change the light in your home. Wide open blinds! Blast-wash your home with light. Your ideas are there. Let them cut into your dance! This is like a daily sword-polishing devotion. There is a discipline of the ritual in plants that the ACE OF SWORDS lives by. First year, roots. Second year, foliage. Third year, fruits and flowers. It is recommended to explore this natural discipline of how plants live and develop. Let it come to flower in the patience of your daily devotion.

Stick to the point to cut through any trouble. Breath is both prayer and passion here.

The Ace of Swords
Sticking to the point, cutting through, quickening

Enter The Ace of Swords

Welcome to SWORDS! This is the place within Mystereum for you to see and feel how your communications can cut right through like a sprout that bursts into the sun. And, you have met THE SUN. My, is he bright like you! I am like a single sunbeam. He is like all of your brightness. Let us focus shall we?!

I love to stick to the point and keep things clear. I think ideas will stand up for themselves like sprouts that burst into the sun. Remember that when a sprout bursts up into the sun, it may not know where it is. Remember my brother, the ACE OF WANDS, as you think about how the sprout naturally placed itself. I want to show you how natural ideas cut right through when you are aware to notice detail. This occurs even when you have no certainty of your placement.

I love to meditate my options and be objective before I take my next step. THE EMPEROR came here and gifted me that. I love to identify, understand, and feel my causes. The QUEEN OF WANDS gifted me that. I love to trust my personal convictions. TEMPERANCE taught me that. I love to cut through the bull while I protect my privacy. We can thank the QUEEN OF SWORDS for that one! I learned my speed and agility from Mr. CHARIOT.

Then something happened. I had already been heated and cooled and rolled and hammered with diligence and patience for a long time. I was then annealed, heated to glow, and then came the tempering. I was a sword after all. The tempering and quickening were things I wanted. What happened is that I hesitated. After all this work on me, I was held at my hottest point over brisk and cool water. Fortunately, my sis, the ACE OF CUPS, had provided all the water. I was to be quenched to quicken me. I was to be thrust at my hottest temperature into the cold water. What if I cracked? What if I. . .Let us stop right there.

See how easy it is to build bad drama with one worry after I had been through so much? I like thicker dramas than that. Heck, I had been through all the other parts. What was I worried about? Here is what it was. After all the hard work and all the studious efforts, I was to be thrust into an unknown. That unknown made me who I am today! So, like stepping onto the stage for the first time, IN I WENT HOT into the coldest of water pssssshhhhhhhzzzzssssssss! Not a crack anywhere. In fact, that may still be the most favorite speaking engagement I have had where I just went right in and was quenched. And, all I said was pssssshhhhhhhzzzzssssssss!, and POOF I was me!

So, after all this, I want to tell you one thing. If you work hard and go step by step, AND have a positive feeling, even a positive unknown of a feeling, and a certain single step is unsure, meditate your options without hurry or worry. Meditate to decide how to act. Sometimes, like with my quenching, that last 5 percent of the time felt like the OTHER 95 percent of the time. More came together in one step than all the previous steps. But, in came the 2 OF WANDS to teach me not to perceive many little things as one big thing. I took that to heart and was quenched in the sword-making water. After that I decided not to let one new step get missed. Here's the catch. I KNEW where that water came from. It was good water from a good cup. I knew the diligence and patience that created me up to that point. I took a risk, just like those sprouts do when they burst into the sun unsure of where they are. That thought keeps me sharp now when I come to an unknown step.

mentioned that it is okay to jump ahead to get a sense of her first. Just look in on her without words. There is no rush. With your imagination, I would like you to present her a weightless gift when you arrive there after going step by step from here. She has a vast collection of sharp ideas. She asked me to tell you that she would like you to tell her one of yours when you are ready.

⇒ *IMAGINATION TOOLS*
FROM THE ACE OF SWORDS

- I gift you the ability to cut to the chase, to the core idea, and stick to it. Bet it will show you the way to sync up almost every time with a proper and sharp focus in your perspective.
- I would like you to make a single gift of your own creation for yourself, and place it somewhere prominent.

You have come a long way. Hope you enjoy Mystereum, your Imagination Tools, and especially your imagination. I want you to have your own quenching of sorts here. Pause. As you move along use your imagination to come up with a gift for The QUEEN OF SWORDS for when you meet her. It is all YOU! Use your imagination! She

The 2 of Swords

The 2 OF SWORDS indicates a balance of opposites in a decision to be made soon. Consideration of others' views is also indicated. Judge clearly whether a shout or a whisper of an action will be heard more clearly. Discern the parts of the decision. No action may be necessary at all, and that may even have a greater impact!

Enter The 2 of Swords

COOL! You just showed up like we do as we focus on clear ideas when they come together! Come on in! You have probably seen this symbol with four gold pillars throughout Mystereum. We are ideas here that come together and communicate a clear focus. See a perspective that no one else has, like how we highlight the one pillar. Its color changed when we focused on it. We like laughing it up with the 5 and 7 OF WANDS about this kind of perspective. They full on get us!

Notice how we focus on the four-pillared symbol here. Oh, by the way what is the 4 four-pillared symbol, you might ask? Cool! We will tell you what we know. We have not left Mystereum. So, we cannot tell you who or what made or brought that symbol here. But, we know this. It started in

The 2 of Swords
Balanced opposites, upcoming decisions

an imagination. And, from some faraway world there were these people called Egyptians. They came before us. They had a symbol with 4 pairs of barley stalks that lean together in four pairs on the common base of the ground. We are pretty dang sure that the imagination that cooked us up let the soul of T. S. Elliott be the guide and outright stole the Egyptian's symbol, made it look like this, and turned it into gold. The original symbol was called a hieroglyph to the Egyptians. Spelled like HIEROPHANT. Hieroglyphs bring the voice and meaning in with a picture. Here, this symbol is the basis of Mystereum. It means "Fabric." Four pairs of two's that come together on a common ground that is our community. Could be 4 sets of people in a community. Or, it can also be the ideas you put together in your imagination that come out from the common ground of your creativity! Pretty cool, huh?! We dig it immensely!

There is always a lot for us to say BEFORE we focus as balanced opposites here. It takes a lot to get simple sometimes. But, we will now get right to it. See how when we focus on the four-pillared symbol the area of our focus is highlighted? See how it appears different? We do not really think this means the symbol is blue. But, when we look this closely, we find a whole world within the area of our focus that is subtly different from the original world around it. Pan in and out in your imagination and see what you see! See how your focus can change things and inform you.

We love a balance of opposites that illuminates a decision in places that look pretty much the same if you have not focused in on them. We are about the connective tissue of your ideas. We are about the things that communicate areas to focus on in your imagination. We always consider others' views. Sometimes that is all we do. We only include what we feel communicates our focus the best. This helps us make thoughtful decisions and enjoy them more. We can express the thought behind our decisions when we see our focus clearly. Sometimes no action is necessary at all. But, we like to prepare ourselves with focused study. That prepares our way as we move along.

➣ IMAGINATION TOOL
FROM THE TWO OF SWORDS

- We gift you the tool to focus for better communication. Study things so that you can strongly see and discover the way you were naturally born to see. Your decisions help you see how you see. That way you can be strong and clear and simple when you express yourself.

The 3 of Swords

The 3 OF SWORDS indicates the refraction when you experience distorted feelings. Sense any distortion that you feel as the illusion of a twig put into clear water. Watch the illusion. The twig of your emotions is not really bent under the water. Remove what is unnatural from your emotions. Express the expectations of your blind spots to yourself, or to a friend. Operating heavy machinery is not suggested at this time. Take care of yourself AS the heavy machinery. Flow through change and be honest when you express yourself. Forget. It is certainly often for getting here!

The 3 OF SWORDS indicates distortion of feelings, the illusion of a twig into water, a heartfelt refraction. Your expectations may be big blind spots at this time. Take a walk. Then relax as you flow through the change born when you forget. Lighten up. Literally, lighten your load. There is clarity to find here even though it may feel as if this pain will never end. Take a walk in the park. Look more than both ways when you cross the street. It is indicated that you move in a way you are not used to or that is uncomfortable. No one said this one is going to be easy. Piece by piece. Step by step. Breath by breath. Breathe deeply. Breath by breath you will clear things up.

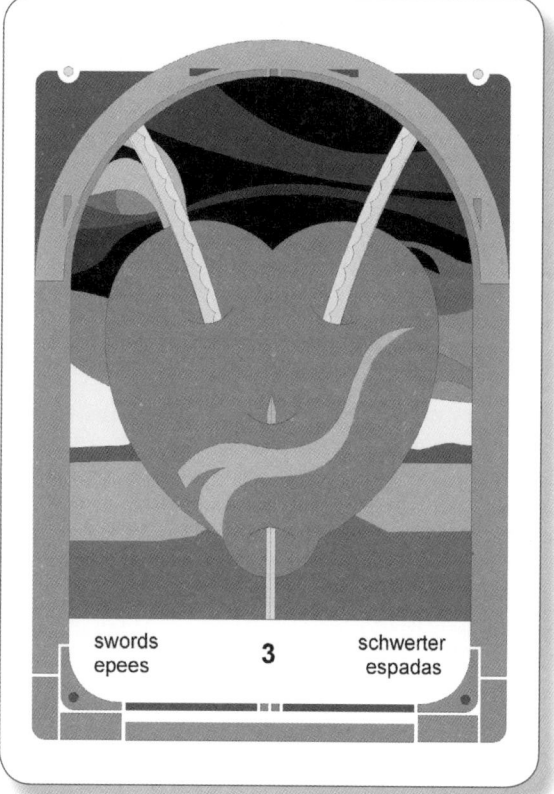

The 3 of Swords
Refraction, distorted feelings, moving slowly

Enter The 3 of Swords

Welcome. Move slow. Nothing is as it seems here. There is a magic of emotions, but not always in a very fun way to start. Our part of Mystereum is where things appear distorted. With a little perspective, shift! Think of a twig. When you put part of it underwater it seems to bend at the surface. Try it before we move on. Your finger in a cup of water will do. We want to make sure you can take proper care here. A toothbrush in water works, too. We will wait. We feel this is important for you to see. This place is an important one for careful attention. Be mindful with your emotions.

Now that you are back remember that twig or finger or toothbrush you used to see it bend when it went underwater. You see, there are times when our emotions are distorted, too. Then the imagination starts to twist and get tight and hard to use. It is like you are in two places at once, kind of split. We want to offer that when you feel perplexed, or like you simply cannot get a handle on things and it hurts, slow down and breathe. As you breathe, begin to flex your imagination. Do not try to move it at first. Simply flex it back and forth. Flex a little bigger, a little smaller. Once you have warmed it up a little, try and flex it to change your perspective and PULL that twig out of the water. It might not be so bent after all.

We are kind of like the quicksand of Mystereum. We are what we are. And, we want you to know our tricks so it becomes more play for you when you feel out of sorts. Simple, small, flex movements to begin in your imagination here. Simple movements until you feel your perspective begin to shift. It is important to take stock here pronto when things are distorted or feelings that perplex or confuse you come up. We have not built much here. But, we have heard rumors that when lots of us get together over time left unchecked something called THE TOWER is formed. Maybe when you pass by next time you can let us know what you have seen on your journey.

We love to express expectations as big ole blind spots. We take care in these times to try not to be too nimble. We are clear to take care and look before each step. We breathe deeply until these perplexed feelings subside.

We DO, though, love to flow through this change. We learn from it. Forgetting is rockin' for getting here!

⇒ IMAGINATION TOOLS
FROM THE THREE OF SWORDS

- We gift you the tool to stop when you feel things are distorted. Breathe and move to let them go to get clarity. Remember what you learn from this when it occurs. Write it down.
- We gift you that we are the shell of the seed when it cracks open underground.

The 4 of Swords

The 4 OF SWORDS indicates your thoughts have come to fruition to give you a space where they can grow. This is a time of preparation. Grow your diamond out of your rough times. Here, never hurry, and never rest. Pace. Enhance your preparedness. Do not lock your muscles into play. Direct a calm flow where things can grow. Good opportunities are ahead. Use discretion in how you deal with things that are present. Literally, tell yourself, "Take care."

Enter The 4 of Swords

Well, you sure got through that last patch of quicksand great! You are here! You are where the strengths of your solid and well-placed new energies communicate well. Express your ideas in motion! Let 'em flow as they cut through in motion. Feel your imagination as the lead edge of a ship at sea on a sunny day with a good wind! This lead edge of a ship is called a prow. Let your imagination keep pull-cutting you through as you enjoy the wind of your ideas in your hair! If we see clearly, you clip right along with your ideas!

Our motion is about thoughts that come to fruition. It is about an idea that you manifest. We love this kind of place to fuel you as you express and communicate ideas with strength in motion!

The 4 of Swords
Fruition, communication in motion

There is preparation time planted here where great things can grow. We work the soil. You got out of the 3s distortion, so you have another tool you can plant here. Love to grow your diamond even in your rough times. It lives and grows simply by your thoughts. You need not lock your muscles into play here. Your communication is more fluid and natural. It simply flows!

➢ IMAGINATION TOOL
FROM THE FOUR OF SWORDS

- We gift you the tool to plan preparations and grow your imagination wonderfully. Planning can sometimes be another invisible support. Remember, also, that your warm-up may not often be a part of your performance!

The 5 of Swords

The 5 OF SWORDS indicates a sense of defeat. You may feel overwhelmed. Ignore your ego if it throws a tantrum. Wash up on your own shore after your storm has broken. Feel the calm AFTER your storm. Careful reassessments and subtle movements are indicated to get out of this heart knot. Wipe your brow and move forward slowly with big breaths.

Beware of truth-against-the-world kinds of thinking where everything is out to get you or there is no way out. That may be simply fear and ego-echoes tantrum-ing through what may be depression or low energy. Rest well. Remember that some people feel that the ego can only tantrum for 2 minutes (plus or minus) at a time. Ride it out. Two minutes of breathing. Right now it is indicated that the ego's low endurance may deal you successive strikes out of desperation.

Weather this storm as inner weather that makes your outer situation. Cease pity. DO NOT return the ego-echo's call! Feel that! With some careful reassessment and a good bout of fictional beliefs dropped, you will be free to accomplish your visualized outcomes again before too long. Go get the oil changed in your car if it is time. Tighten the chain on your bike. Empathize with those processes. Google it. You might just feel like you have exploded. There WAS calm before the storm. You will MAKE calm again as it becomes AFTER the storm. Do it differently the second time, though.

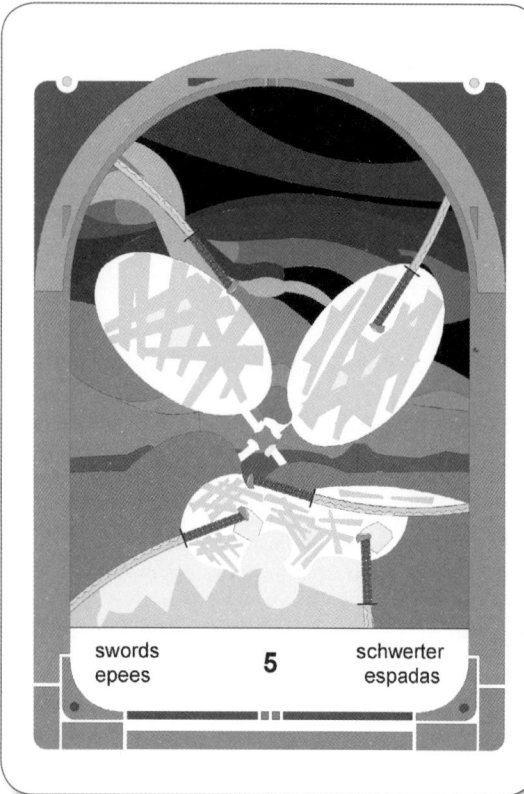

The 5 of Swords
Careful reassessments, subtle movements

The landscape may be a little different after a storm and a chain tightening. It is indicated to get back a positive grip on your ideas.

Also, think about it this way: If you split wood with an adze and it gets stuck in a knot, all work is stopped. Stop pulling the adze. Stop whacking. Tap your adze softly and consistently moving it here and there. You will get yourself out of your heart knot and wipe your brow soon enough.

Enter The 5 of Swords

Rest! You ran right through your 4 OF SWORDS and communicated in motion. Rest. Take a breather. Otherwise your tired self might start to feel defeated! We do not want that. We want you to feel your fatigue, and that maybe you feel your ideas are scattered everywhere. Almost like you fell when you were too tired and they spilled everywhere. No matter. Let your ideas have their own picnic as you rest and relax away from them. You may have spilled them so you can look at them differently before you begin to pick them up again.

Is there an overwhelming sense of defeat here? Did that defeat come from too hard a push? Did it come from a "truth against the world" kind of thinking where you were being stubborn because you were tired? While you rest please feel free to ignore the ego tantrum-ing for two minutes at each successive strike at your ideas. They need to rest, too. They may be hyper-tired. It is suggested to give your ideas a good nap.

Self pity is not allowed in this place. We like you too much ALL the time to let that hullaballoo creep into your imagination. Know that to be effective do just enough right now! We suggest to carefully re-assess things after you rest from this chaos and hullaballoo. There will be a calm after the storm. If you like to split wood, simply tap the adze in a different way lightly and slowly rock it back and forth to get out of any heart knots. Once you do, wipe your brow. That is all we have for you. Rest well.

⇒ IMAGINATION TOOL
FROM THE FIVE OF SWORDS

- We gift you the tool of rest and very subtle actions for your imagination when you are tired.
- We gift you a nap if you would like it. Do not nap to avoid something. Nap to rest and reset your clarity. Remember the 3 OF SWORDS there. The 4 OF SWORDS is a cool bridge. We are here on the other side.

The 6 of Swords

The 6 OF SWORDS indicates baggage from the past or problems that have been dwelt on at length. Identify any negative beliefs you have. Begin not to depend on them. Look around and see what the world has to offer. This is like the day AFTER a big storm. Face your problems. Know it is time to fight them off. Exchange them. See what is really there then! Give and exchange from THAT perspective. Amend your inner soil by simply letting go of baggage. The Universe loves presents and surprises. It re-gifts back great ones! Gift your baggage to the Universe by raising your hands and opening them and thinking of a bird that flies away free.

Un cadeau. A present. Send out a box to be opened. Open your hands raised high. See what the world has to offer. Expectations can dull your senses. Some expectations make you more effective, though. This happens when they take care of things outside your focus in a natural way. See what IS rather than what you expect things to be. Sometimes all of your problems may not be problems at all. Before you jettison any, take a look and see how all things work together. A disassembled car in a garage can be a mess. The key there is just another part. But, put together, and that key = VROOOOOM! There is also the other side. There is the time to take out the trash of pieces that do not fit. Be mindful not to trick yourself to think things work when they do

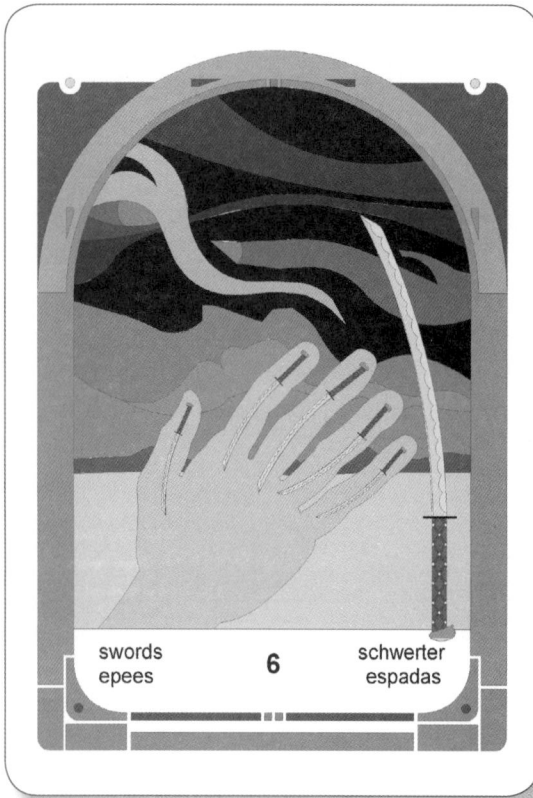

The 6 of Swords
Letting go of baggage, presents, surprises

not. Remember that the re-assembled car with several extra pieces in your hand might not = VROOM! In that case find the trash can or look at how things go together again.

Enter The 6 of Swords

Start talkin'! Express those ideas! We want to hear them! Now is a great time to express them. Go for it! This is the place where you are probably full of them! Do not reach for more. You will get too full. That might just hurt inside as your other ideas begin to feel crowded.

You have everything you need here. You have a full hand of ideas to work with. Express those ideas out loud before you go any further. Write them down or sketch them or both. Maybe all you need are diagrams right now. Bring your ideas to work in front of you in a variety of ways. If you have already been doing this, begin to fill in each one more fully so you more clearly see them.

Drop things from the past. Some are oftentimes problems that you may have thought about for quite a while. After you express them, identify expectations you have about them. This way you will not need to depend on them. Open your eyes and see them. See what the world has to offer for your ideas in a new way.

This is the place to face problems and know when it is time to fight them off by working them. Work the problem. This is also the place to love to explore what your ideas are!

➣ *Imagination Tool*
From The Six of Swords

- We gift you the tool of a portal, a doorway from your imagination out into the reality right in front of you. Count roll with your ideas. Are they all present? Any napping? This doorway likes you to bring the ideas that are awake through.

The 7 of Swords

The 7 of Swords indicates something sneaky and devious and sly and stealthy that most probably hides right in plain sight in front of you. Look at things a different way. Pause. Expand outward through blind spots past where they deceive you! Identify mirages. Mirror them and play along just a little to draw them out of sight. Send them away forgotten. Hide in plain sight as you do this. Begin to move past them as you send them away! It is indicated that you are not as exposed as you feel.

Your troubles may be what hide in plain sight. Underhanded things like theft, robbery, unreliability, betrayal, spying, dishonor, deceit, and suspicion can be indicated. These are kind of sensational things. Look differently. Pause and expand past them. Schedule a day off in the middle of the week to shake up your schedule and shake out unnecessary pieces. Feel into blind spots. See the hand and seventh sword that hides in plain sight in the card. Feel that when you hide in plain sight! You are GONE and THERE at the same time. You are everywhere to be seen, and nowhere to be found. A good and fun game of hide and seek might release some troubles. Play hide and seek with your ideas. Feel your place, not your clever. The card does not indicate your path, here. YOU DO! Toss some stones into a bush and watch as they disappear. Stand and deliver in a new way! That can make your ideas immune to deception. Silence can also provide deliverance here. Discern between the negativity of when no one notices you versus the same thing as positive which indicates your stealth. Visualize isolation versus solitude. Does one feel better than the other?

Enter The 7 of Swords

See anything? Where's the 7ᵀᴴ Sword? Where's the hand? Are the 6 swords together really swords? This is a place of sneaky and devious and sly and stealthy things. Troubles often hide in plain sight here. This is the place in Mystereum to learn to look at what IS. Disregard your expectations here. Take a fresh look. You may want to look for more than one thing here to practice feeling the whole scene.

We pause and expand here before we move as we feel our blind spots! We do not have to see them. If we feel something is there, we find it an action. We love to hide in plain sight, too. It can be kind of fun on the hide-and-seek flipside. Here, we enjoy that we are often not as exposed as we feel. We are certainly no less aware, though. Use all your communication senses here. Pick several Imagination Tools to help you discover something.

The 7 of Swords
Sneaky, stealthy, hiding in plain sight

➣ *Imagination Tools*
From The Seven of Swords

- We gift you a tool to clear out hindrances to your good ideas that are invisible but hide in plain sight!
- We gift to you a tool to play and remove yourself from situations in your mind to engage differently as you shift your perspective and re-engage.

The 8 of Swords

The 8 of Swords indicates a positive change of mind that manifests towards your troubles. Be bold and enhance this positive change of mind with the justice of your material progress. See your health in a new way. Act in the moment. Release yourself from the prison of any false beliefs that were born of expectation.

It is indicated that you release yourself from what you learned with our 7. This is an important lesson. Act in the moment free of expectations. Your sense of meaning will be felt in your actions.

Enter The 8 of Swords

So, you saw right through those things that linger and can trip you up! Congrats! Now, you can jump forth and begin to express your dynamic ideas. A positive change of mind is easier to feel and shift with! Enjoy this positive change of mind. Be creative and dynamic as you focus on any troubles one by one. Keep them on the move in your idea solar system. Freshen them with transformation. Move them right out of your scene if you feel to do so. Some of them may become valuable assets when you do not waste trouble and simply work the problem.

The 8 of Swords
Releasing false beliefs, expectation as chaff

You may start to feel the magical scale that Justice gave you more. With this newfound sense of balance feel material progress. Find love for your health in a new way. We are one of the rest stops for THE FOOL. He has brought a great many of his discoveries here. We have many perspectives that communicate together to be experienced as a single group. THE FOOL's discoveries shed light on and release us from the prison of our expectations. We like to call ourselves The Little Anti-TOWER. We live to act in the moment here!

⇒ *IMAGINATION TOOL*
FROM THE EIGHT OF SWORDS

- We gift you the tool to be positive and quick when you adjust your idea solar system. Keep your ideas bold and your imagination healthy!

The 9 of Swords

The 9 OF SWORDS indicates situations or events that near completion. They also indicate another plateau that arrives. Remember the mountain park of a false summit. Feel experience AS the situation. Have you passed through the mental anguish of false summits before?

Though misery, suffering, and desolation may be present the 9 OF SWORDS loves that the path is clear. False summits and immediate horizons are seen as trail-markers rather than destinations. Progress is being made! This is a place about utilizing the false summit to mark your way. There may be mental anguish until you realize you can move through this place. You are not stopped by it. Take care as you move forward.

Understand the false summit of a mountain climb as a trail-marker of progress and an immediate horizon rather than a destination. Pass through this time, through your false summits. Do not judge yourself. That weighs you down. Sprint through! Find enjoyment in the scenery, but hoof it until you get back to the next part of your process!

This is one of those places where people of the land's wisdom shines. We call it Zen Master Farmer's wisdom. Here is a piece. If you realize you are in a hole and cannot get out, stop digging! A shovel is an indelicate tool for this time. Visualize your experience AS the situation. Own up and try a new perspective, and get back on course.

The 9 of Swords
Nearing completions, dynamic plateaus

Enter The 9 of Swords

You have come to a plateau of how you express your ideas. You are no longer on a climb. It is time to feel the groups of your ideas just as YOU do in this higher place along the way. Pause and reflect here. Put together how you want to express the particular way you have grouped the things you do. Express your ideas about the things you do with feeling! Put it all together here. We do not advise to express your feelings here. We suggest that you infuse your feelings into what is communicated by your actions so that they are natural. Your actions will express them just fine. We love that if you feel your experience AS the situation here, you will be wonderfully prepared as each new plateau opens up for you.

Pause. Feel how you have arrived again. Get a new handle on how you express what you do. Make a clear path. Each false summit brings a new, immediate horizon to remember as a trail-marker of your progress. Remember that you are no more at the mercy of your past than you are of old photo albums. Commend yourself on your progress. Find the pictures in your scene that you want to take forward.

⇒ *IMAGINATION TOOL* FROM THE NINE OF SWORDS

- We gift you the tool of commencement. We bring you the gift of commencement as a pause before you expand further along your travels. You have graduated here! We feel that your masteries will lead you to exciting discoveries!

The 10 of Swords

The 10 OF SWORDS indicates ruin and anguish, both physical pain and otherwise. Also it is indicated to realize that the worst has already passed. Rock bottom is a strong place to stand. Remember that. Rock bottom is a strong place to stand. Plant your feet strongly on the solid ground and look up! Anything visible is probably something better. Know that you have pulled through. Take a big breath. Phewww!

The 10 OF SWORDS is similar to THE TOWER. But, the worst is indicated to have already passed here. Take another big breath! Also indicated is to develop and understand through curiosity and analysis. Thorough creativity is present and in your vision. Now is the time you can penetrate through to the truth or essence of a thing or situation. Will it to appear as you release blocks. Mental facility and skill are indicated to increase as you release ideas that no longer work

Enter The 10 of Swords

We feel ruin and anguish here. We feel both physical pain and pain inside. We love, though, that the worst has already passed. We love that anything visible is probably something better. We do not just jump at anything, though. We love that we have pulled through.

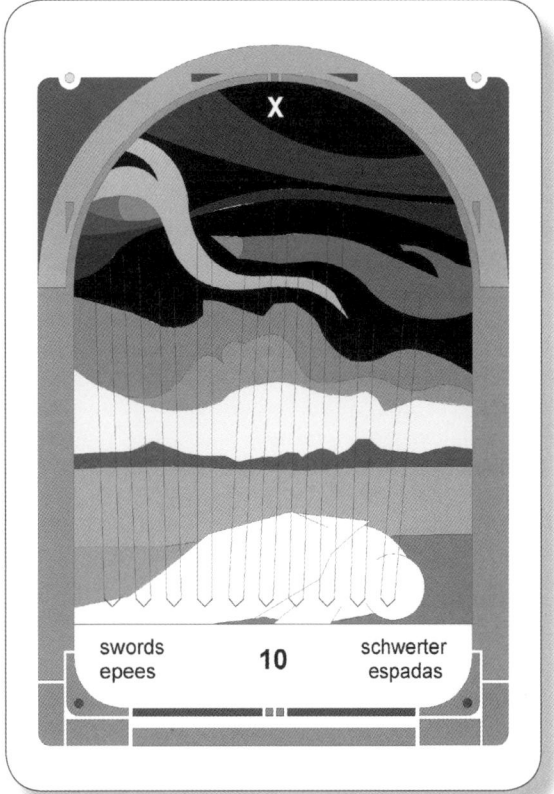

The 10 of Swords
Anguish, release, essence

You see, we love to realize and release pain and distortions! We love to release with big breaths! Phewww, we MADE IT! Remember your great wind!

We love that though we may be on rock bottom, we have been taught to keep a fresh perspective before, during, and after our storm. We love that though we stand on rock bottom, rock bottom is a DANG strong place to support our feet! Keep going slowly! Take big breaths! You can DO IT!

➢ IMAGINATION TOOL
FROM THE TEN OF SWORDS

- We gift you the tool to feel your feet on solid ground. Release pain you have when you are ready. Forget. What is the lesson here?

The Page of Swords

The PAGE OF SWORDS indicates to find yourself curious to understand new developments. It is indicated that now is the time to penetrate through to the truth or essence of a situation. Have playful creativity with all that you experience. You may receive news of an aHA nature! You have a great ability to communicate your ideas with a newfound zeal. This may be what brings you to receive some news.

Enter The Page of Swords

I AM the PAGE OF SWORDS.

I love to be curious about and come to understand new developments. I love the curiosity and analysis you bring forth into YOUR ROYAL COURT.

I love that your thorough creativity and vision now penetrates through to express the truth and essence of things and situations.

I love that you have the thoughtful courage to express your truths.

I love that your mental facility and skill develops. Express your expert skill in simple play and when you communicate your ideas.

I love that you receive and bring news of your new expressions to Your Royal Court.

⇒ *Imagination Tool*
From The Page of Swords

- I gift you a tool to balance your discoveries with your Crown chakra and the 10 of Wands at the same time. May your idea solar system be brightly balanced on its sharpest edge with no hands. All on its own may it permeate Your Royal Court with clear expression!

The Page of Swords
Curiosity, new developments, zeal

The Knight of Swords

The Knight of Swords indicates that you generate ideas and love to be placed well to incorporate them. With any opposition large or small, your conviction in your beliefs and ideas is very alive. It is also indicated to defend what you stand for. To put ideas into action is the focus here! Be prepared to defend their placement and their positions. Full speed ahead Bay-BEE! Your ideas work with a strong base here.

Enter The Knight of Swords

I AM the Knight of Swords.

I love being a generator of ideas and placed well to incorporate them.

I love to put my ideas into action.

I love that with opposition large or small, my conviction in my beliefs and ideas is very alive.

I defend my stance if necessary. With "Full speed ahead!" I make my ideas so!

The Knight of Swords
Generating ideas, being well-placed, incorporating

I love the agility I have across the board when I brace my feet against a strong foundation and hop and skip and leap!

I love that my communications are natural and that I express them in my actions.

➣ IMAGINATION TOOL
FROM THE KNIGHT OF SWORDS

- I gift you a tool to incorporate your discoveries using THE MOON, THE STAR, THE SUN, THE CHARIOT, STRENGTH, JUDGMENT, THE 4 OF SWORDS, and THE 10 OF WANDS. They make a great team! May you awaken with magical renewal in your balance! Use this tool to present and incorporate your discoveries into the celestial light of YOUR ROYAL COURT!

The Queen of Swords

The QUEEN OF SWORDS indicates shrewdness and loves to hold back her opinions until she says just exactly what needs to be said. She has a constitution of love, intelligence, and professionalism. She makes her opinions perfectly clear. It is also indicated here that you will see right through any lies or unnecessary things. Evaluate the truth of what you carefully notice in your situation. Present your ideas in a simple way that is clear and direct. Be straight up! Present your ideas with no NO BULLPOOPY!

Enter The Queen of Swords

I AM the QUEEN OF SWORDS.

I am shrewd and judicious. From me no news is just as good as good news. Worry has no place here.

I hold back my opinions until I say *exactly* what needs to be said. Period. Always. No need to hold your breath.

I love it when your constitution makes your opinions crystal clear. That makes me smile. Period. Always.

The Queen of Swords
Shrewdness, exact statements, clear opinions

I love when you use your fine intelligence and clear voice to present yourself in the most effective ways.

I see right through lies as they are being presented. A strong silence while I listen is often my first response. It is okay to say, "I do not believe you."

I incorporate my truth in situations. I am clear and direct in the way that is best suited to the situation and my truth.

I am the voice of your reason when fully thought out and expressed in a clear and direct way. Fit, finish, and polish are not of concern to me. They are required.

➢ IMAGINATION TOOL
FROM THE QUEEN OF SWORDS

- I gift you the tool of the idea to be effective when you present yourself. With this you can stand your ground with positive and confident gestures. I do not move out of the way. Also, when I am clear and direct, people rarely take aim. ☺

The King of Swords

The KING OF SWORDS indicates you discern with a clarity of perception while you are also logical and fair. Here you do not allow emotions to interfere with your abilities to bring beliefs and often very innovative ideals to fruition. You are careful to weigh all of the angles of a situation to make a fair decision. Your decision is fitting for all involved like JUSTICE. Cunning and cleverness are never present here.

Explore the differences between equanimity and equality. Your clarity can go beyond your spoken words.

Also, a tendency to be emotionally detached is indicated. Mind that you do not make those around you feel intellectually inferior. Respect YOUR ROYAL COURT as you lead it. Be mindful not to overuse your cerebral ability. Avoid cunning and outsmarting people. Do not allow ideas that are clever to get in your way. Wave your hand. Feel and act after you listen. It is indicated that your clarity and effectiveness go beyond the words you speak.

Enter The King of Swords

I AM the KING OF SWORDS.

I am careful to weigh all angles of a situation before I act.

The King of Swords
Clarity of perception, discerning, logical and fair

I love to be logical and fair. My perceptions are clear. I discern well.

I do not allow emotions to interfere with my abilities to bring my beliefs and innovative ideals to fruition.

I make fair decisions that befit each and all involved. All benefit when my decisions befit the situation.

I exclude cunning and clever ideas from touching anyone.

I have a clarity that goes beyond my spoken words.

☞ *Imagination Tool*
From The King of Swords

- I gift you the clearest and most effective communications within and outside all of Your Royal Court. May you use these to carry Your Royal Court to your highest purpose.
These are the things I wish for you.

You are blessed and sacred. That is part of your inner inheritance.

The keys to all of your kingdom of The Land of Mystereum are now all yours!

Poof!!
The Fool here!
I did it! I Poofed!
I have invited everyone together for you!

ENTER ALL MYSTEREUM CHARACTERS!

From all of Us and the whole Land of Mystereum! We are all the experiences of THE FOOL.

We are honored to have you here! Your presence and insight has been most appreciated. We love the imagination that only you bring! We love that your imagination is like no other, and is extra special!

We wish you smilingly-effective creativity, an infinitely expansive imagination, and lots of fun and adventure along your way as you discover many new things as you create more uses for your imagination tools on your journey.

You are blessed and sacred. We look forward to you personalizing your Imagination Tools! Wishin' you WOO HOO FOR YOU as you explore and discover and create and make rockin' things with your ideas and imagination, and your idea solar system and Imagination Tools!

Namaste,
All The Best Light n Lightning,
Mystereum

Appendix

IMAGINATION TOOL CHEAT SHEET

Mystereum suggests to begin your readings with these concepts to draw your Imagination Tools into your reading. Write 2 to 4 short action statements that come to mind for each Imagination Tool in your reading. We find this helps begin the process to transform your reading into actionable tasks, and bring your ideas and projects to life.

The Mystereum Tarot Card Back
Meditate. Contemplate. Meditate.

Archetypal Imagination
Major Arcana. Big ideas. Inspire.

Grounding Imagination
Pentacles. Earth. Ground. Foundation. Solid.

Fulfilling Imagination
Cups. Water. Flow. Emotions. Nourish.

Energizing Imagination
Wands. Fire. Energy. Activate. Invigorate passion.

Communicative Imagination
Swords. Air. Communicate.

Archetypal Imagination is about The Major Arcana with big ideas.

Grounding Imagination is about Pentacles with solid things that you can touch.

Fulfilling Imagination is about Cups with flow and how you feel.

Energizing Imagination is about Wands with energy that invigorates you.

Communicative Imagination is about Swords with communication and how you interact.

***

All cards, both the Major Arcana and the Minor Arcana, come from The Fool's experiences on the journey.

Part One

Archetypal Imagination

The FOOL's Journey Through the MAJOR ARCANA

Ø The Fool ∞
   Natural expression. Feelings. Journey. New directions. Castle of memory.

I The Magician
   Arche. First spark. Original idea. Intense focus. Inception. Flash. House of creativity.

II The High Priestess
   Techne. Intuition. Inner illumination. Conception. Unrevealed influences. Giving form.

III The Empress
   Carries to full term. Gives ideas life. Abundance. Sensuality. Earthly gifts. Golden glow. HANGED MAN's mom.

IV The Emperor

Establish place. Oversee. Order. Natural world. Step by step. Placement. Idea Solar System. Sense of orbits.

V The Hierophant

Mindbodybeautiful. Seat for your mind. Tradition. Wise. Soothing spirit to earth. Crown portal. Temple of body. Inner light. Inner strength.

VI The Lovers

Heart. Vibrant joinery. Vitality. Mutual witness. Enhance. Fabric. Love what you love. Bow and arrow together.

VII The Chariot

Agility. Power of speed. Power of Wow! Strategy like sunflowers. Synchronized. YAH breathing. Performance.

VIII Justice

Magical inner scale. Balance. Fair. Befit. Considerate. Mindful. Inner scale. Equilibrium.

IX The Hermit

Inner activity. Magical cloister of mind. Fresh mysteries. Inner lantern.

X The Wheel

Imagination Toolbox.

XI Strength

Strong calm place.

XII The Hanged Man

A place of your own to float. Illumination. Place of no resistance for your Idea Solar System. Perspective for play.

XIII Death

Forgetting is for getting.

XIV Temperance

Freedom to see bigger things. You are a wonderful, uniquely complete being. Meet your support.

XV The Devil

Freedom to feel your desires clearly. Explore them and strike your own balances as you do no harm. Visit THE HANGED MAN. VROOM!

XVI The Tower

Be fully present and protected as you weather big storms of change. Powerful silence. Leave the lightning. Keep the truth.

XVII The Star

Eternal glimmers of hope. Vivid imagination to find your cosmic groove! A gift of directions. Light up your ideas.

XVIII The Moon

Bright eyes in the night. Magnetize your ideas. Light your way. Magnetic smiles direct like a compass.

XIX The Sun

The true, inner inheritance were born with. YOU! Discover your inner riches! Refresh yourself with a stretch. Shine and rest and dream with actions.

XX Judgment

YOU are the gardener of your soul and your body and your life. Only accept and give good back like in a garden. To amend your soil. Use your anticipation and patience to see new sprouts of ideas.

XXI The World

Mastery leads to further discovery. Play with your imagination. Celebrate your discoveries! The Portal of the Seamless Segue.

Part Two

Grounding Imagination

The Fool's Journey Through Pentacles

The Ace of Pentacles
Sense inner inheritances. Focus and tend to your ideas from their first sprout. Forget bad habits. Increase the potential of your ideas. Grow a whole idea solar system from a single idea.

The 2 of Pentacles
Strive for equality, equanimity. A direct line from your feet to your imagination. Ground-grabbers. Imagine things as soon as they touch your feet.

The 3 of Pentacles
Perceive positive groups. Bring your ideas to reality.

The 4 of Pentacles
Hidden supports always present. Structure your imagination. Magical ground.

The 5 of Pentacles
Your imagination is a warm and established inner light. Make more room for good stuff.

The 6 of Pentacles
Orbits for your ideas in your idea solar system.

The 7 of Pentacles
A place above everything for your imagination to expand.

The 8 of Pentacles
A portal for a perfect doorway. 8 is like the infinity symbol ∞ turned. Rotate to expand as ∞.

The 9 of Pentacles
Your ideas work together wonderfully. Feel this and it is so!

The 10 of Pentacles
Enhance and reinforce and strengthen your sense of fresh and new perspectives. Look forward to YOUR ROYAL COURT.

The Page of Pentacles
Bring forth your discoveries. Group THE MAGICIAN, THE HIEROPHANT, and THE CHARIOT together. Take a field trip and make an Imagination Tool for yourself from your experience.

The Knight of Pentacles
Incorporate your discoveries into your idea solar system. Incorporate things at your own speed. The earth is both active and alive.

The Queen of Pentacles
A vibrant, inner garden to be nourished and tended. All the things you value. An exquisite place.

The King of Pentacles
The totality of the place of YOUR ROYAL COURT. From here you can fly as high as your roots go deep.

Part Three

Fulfilling Imagination
The Fool's Journey Through Cups

The Ace of Cups
Bright eyes to trust your ideas. Smile when you feel fresh ideas at play. Express them.

The 2 of Cups
Another big, bright-eyed smile when you think of your identity. Love yourself. Love your imagination. Love who you are.

The 3 of Cups
Celebrate in your imagination. Celebrate your imagination itself. Celebrate with your imagination. Wiggle and shake around. Dance!

The 4 of Cups
New life to burst forth in your imagination! Enjoy each and every little success.

The 5 of Cups
See hidden treasures. Find safe passage. Emotions wash through like weather.

The 6 of Cups
A balanced and refreshed place to explore and exchange.

The 7 of Cups
A great wind in your imagination to clear the ideas not ready.

The 8 of Cups
Movement to discern things. Paint your whole scene.

The 9 of Cups
A full wreath that always grows around a bright pool. Let your ideas strike chords that resonate.

The 10 of Cups
Feel the strength that shines inside and out.

The Page of Cups
Bring forth your discoveries. Frolic and swim in Your Royal Court!

The Knight of Cups
Trust the depth and strength of your emotions. Connect the depths of your inner world to your sky.

The Queen of Cups
Wisdom of the ages whether you have learned them or not. Act in accord with the wisdom you feel.

The King of Cups
The full love and attention of everything and everyone in Your Royal Court. Magnetic life. Draw in wonderful things.

Part Four

Energizing Imagination

The Fool's Journey

Through Wands

The Ace of Wands

Direct your energies so that you can place them exactly where you feel best. Turn them up and down and find out for yourself what resonates.

The 2 of Wands

Shift your focus and redirect your scale on the fly if you feel perplexed.

The 3 of Wands

Fresh, new, and positive energies from unseen sources. Feel them!

The 4 of Wands

Arrange energy in your imagination with joy. Place your ideas just so. Give them the weight they deserve!

The 5 of Wands

Discover crucial pieces that bring a situation together. Enhance your ability to express the crucial pieces of any situation.

The 6 of Wands

Feel the victory and glory you receive from your ideas!

The 7 of Wands

Fully feel your ideas in action. Take charge and make them real! Be deliberate.

The 8 of Wands

A high level place to play when you are waiting! Enjoy being up in the air from time to time. Make it fun. An active mind is immune to boredom!

The 9 of Wands

Notice and breathe in that wonderfully brief moment of peace and tranquility right before your festivities start up! Complete your work to mark the moment!

The 10 of Wands

Wonderful balance throughout your idea solar system. May you tune and tailor all that is there. Tow your ideas with the grace of your own *mindbodybeautiful*.

The Page of Wands

Birth your discoveries. Bring new energies from deep and dark places into the celestial light of Your Royal Court!

The Knight of Wands

Birth and incorporate your discoveries. Spiritually strengthen.

The Queen of Wands

Your vision is blessed and sacred and magical.

The King of Wands

Complete energies are present. Act in the moment to build.

Part Five

Communicative Imagination
The Fool's Journey
Through Swords

The Ace of Swords
The ability to cut to the chase, to the core idea, and stick to it. Make a single gift of your own creation for yourself. Place it somewhere prominent.

The 2 of Swords
Focus for better communication. Study things. Strongly see and discover the way you were naturally born to see.

The 3 of Swords
Stop when you feel things are distorted. Breathe and move. Feel clearly. Feel the shell of a seed open underground.

The 4 of Swords
Plan preparations. Grow your imagination wonderfully. Your warm-up may not be a part of your performance!

The 5 of Swords
Rest and very subtle actions. A nap to rest and reset your clarity.

The 6 of Swords
A portal from your imagination out into the reality right in front of you. Bring the awake ideas through.

The 7 of Swords
Clear out hindrances to your good ideas. Play and remove yourself from situations to engage differently. Shift your perspective. Re-engage.

The 8 of Swords
Be positive and quick when you adjust your idea solar system.

The 9 of Swords
Commencement. A pause before you expand further. Your masteries will lead you to exciting new discoveries!

The 10 of Swords
Feel your feet on solid ground. Release pain you have when you are ready. Remember the forgetting lesson.

The Page of Swords
Balance your discoveries brightly with clear expression!

The Knight of Swords
Incorporate your discoveries. They make a great team! Awaken magical renewal!

The Queen of Swords
Be effective when you present yourself. Stand your ground with positive and confident gestures.

The King of Swords
The clearest and most effective communications within and outside. You are blessed and sacred. This is a part of your inner inheritance. The keys to your kingdom of The Land of Mystereum are now all yours!

About the Author

Jordan Hoggard graduated from the Texas Tech University College of Architecture with a 5-year professional Bachelor of Architecture degree in 1991 and moved to Denver. He works with Architecture, Art, Feng Shui and Tarot to provide unique, professional services tuned and tailored to his clients' priorities. He currently resides in Santa Fe, New Mexico, with offices in both Santa Fe and Denver.